When Your Child Is Cutting is an excellent resource for both parents and professionals. It presents the facts about cutting and how to manage this problem. It is written in an accessible and readable format. The book takes a good deal of the fear out of dealing with cutting behaviors and provides a needed appendix of frequently asked questions. This text is pragmatic and to the point and can be of real help to many concerned parents and health service providers.

> —Robert W. Motta, Ph.D., ABPP, director of the
> Doctoral Program in School-Community Psychology
> at Hofstra University

I remember the first time I had to say "self-mutilation." I was so naïve. I quickly learned all that this diagnosis entailed. It meant that my daughter and I would be at odds through her early and mid-teens. It meant late night emergency rooms and psychiatric wards. And, for me, it meant anger, guilt, sadness, failure, hopelessness, loneliness—but mostly it meant fear.

But slowly, ever so slowly, the rain stopped, the clouds lifted, and the sun was visible. It has been four and a half years now. The sun shines; my daughter and I walk hand in had. Don't get me wrong. There are cloudy days. But when it rains, my daughter has an umbrella and knows how to use it. The umbrella is the key—not the weather.

First I had to accept my daughter's emotional problems. Then I had to accept and believe that they were real. Then I had to make a commitment to give whatever it took, at whatever cost. But I believed in Dr. McVey. I still have a piece of her note paper hanging on my refrigerator with the words, "This will not last forever."

I believed in her, in my daughter, and in myself. Every month now, without fail, we celebrate the day my daughter stopped cutting. It has been fifty-five months now. And every month is as important as the last.

> —S.S., client of author McVey-Noble

My divorce hit both of my daughters hard. They were two and five at the time. My older daughter later reacted by being afraid of going to school and by expressing other anxiety behaviors. My younger daughter, Nicole, reacted by being the "good little girl." When I had to travel, or when I would come home late after a nighttime presentation for my job, I'd find a paper plate pressed with lipstick-kisses on my pillow. Nicole was five then. During the summer when she was fourteen she began cutting herself.

We tried to get help from a couple of therapists with limited success. Then, as luck—or God—would have it (I truly do believe in divine intervention), I was talking to a colleague who needed to find an alternative school for her daughter. I told her about the school my older daughter went to. She told me her daughter cut herself and gave me Dr. Mcvey's phone number. That's how I found help.

Nicole saw Dr. McVey twice a week. This gave her the support and insights she needed to control the cutting. Dr. McVey encouraged Nicole to call her, even beyond office hours, when she needed her. Nicole learned how to release the pressure valve of her own feelings when they threatened to boil over. She learned to understand her feelings so that she could manage and live with them.

—J.D., client of author McVey-Noble

When Your Child Is Cutting

A Parent's Guide to Helping Children Overcome Self-Injury

MERRY E. M^cVEY-NOBLE, PH.D.

SONY KHEMLANI-PATEL, PH.D.

FUGEN NEZIROGLU, PH.D., ABBP, ABPP

New Harbinger Publications, Inc.

Publisher's Note

This publication is designed to provide accurate and authoritative information in regard to the subject matter covered. It is sold with the understanding that the publisher is not engaged in rendering psychological, financial, legal, or other professional services. If expert assistance or counseling is needed, the services of a competent professional should be sought.

Distributed in Canada by Raincoast Books

Copyright © 2006 by Merry E. McVey-Noble, Sony Khemlani-Patel, and Fugen Neziroglu
New Harbinger Publications, Inc.
5674 Shattuck Avenue
Oakland, CA 94609

Cover design by Amy Shoup; Acquired by Catharine Sutker;
Text design by Tracy Marie Carlson; Edited by Karen O'Donnell Stein

Library of Congress Cataloging-in-Publication Data

McVey-Noble, Merry E.
  When your child is cutting : a parent's guide to helping children overcome self-injury / Merry E. McVey-Noble, Sony Khemlani-Patel, and Fugen Neziroglu.
    p. cm.
  ISBN-13: 978-1-57224-437-5
  ISBN-10: 1-57224-437-2
  1. Self-mutilation—Popular works. 2. Self-injurious behavior—Popular works. I. Khemlani-Patel, Sony. II. Neziroglu, Fugen A., 1951- III. Title.
  RJ506.S44M38 2006
  616.85'82—dc22

                                                    2006010775

New Harbinger Publications' website address: www.newharbinger.com

11   10   09
10   9   8   7   6   5   4

FSC
Mixed Sources
Product group from well-managed
forests and other controlled sources
Cert no. SW-COC-002283
www.fsc.org
© 1996 Forest Stewardship Council

I know that it's been hard for you
To see me act this way
But I don't know what else to do
To convince you to stay . . .
I promise that I'll smile more
If you'd give me one more chance,
We could laugh until our stomachs are sore
You can teach me how to dance

Cause I never meant to
Let you down,
Believe me when I say
I'm sorry

—Anonymous patient

Contents

Acknowledgments   vii

Introduction   1

1
Self-Injury: Just the Facts   19

2
Mind and Body: The Psychological and Biological   33
Bases of Self-Injury

3
Environmental Factors in Self-Injury   47

4

Consequences of Cutting   65

5

How Do I Approach My Child About Cutting?   75

6

Responding to Answers: Common Obstacles to   81
Communication About Self-Injury

7

Psychological Treatment Options   93

8

What to Expect During Treatment   117

9

Supporting Your Child's Recovery   131

10

Specific Skills to Use at Home: Name It, Tame It,   145
Break It Down

APPENDIX

Frequently Asked Questions   155

References   165

I'd like to thank my amazing husband for all of his patience, understanding, love, and wonderful care of our sweet son (along with whom the idea of this book was conceived and developed). I owe tremendous thanks to our incredible baby, whose wonderful disposition and particularly good nature (both in utero and neonatally) allowed me to get a lot of work done at some very unorthodox hours. I'd also like to thank my coauthors for their very hard work and tireless cooperation and support. We would all like to thank our colleagues at New Harbinger, who were patient and provided us with guidance and encouragement. Our editor, Karen Stein, was exceptional. Finally, we'd also like to thank our patients and their parents. They have taught us all the meaning of struggle, but also of hope.

—Merry

I owe a great deal of thanks to my husband for his continual support and enthusiasm and for his extremely thoughtful comments on the manuscript. I have to thank my parents and my in-laws for always lending a hand whenever I needed and for taking such wonderful care of my son while I worked many long hours. We owe a great deal of thanks to Catharine, Heather, and the staff at New Harbinger for allowing us the freedom to complete this book the way we envisioned. Many thanks to our editor, Karen O'Donnell Stein, for her tireless editing and enthusiasm for the project. And finally, to my son, who has made me realize what an exhilarating, scary, and awesome task it is to be a parent!

—Sony

To my husband, Jose A. Yaryura-Tobias, who has always supported my professional growth.

—Fugen

Introduction

From the day our children are conceived, we spend a tremendous amount of time and energy trying to protect them from life's hazards—by immunizing them, watching over them, and teaching them about safety strategies, strangers, first aid, and, as they get older, the dangers of alcohol, drugs, and risky sexual practices. Therefore, it is particularly distressing when your child is hurt or hurting. And it is especially upsetting when your child is hurting herself.

WHAT IS SELF-INJURY?

In this book, we will be addressing self-injury as direct, intentional, repetitive behavior resulting in mild to moderate physical injury (Fauazza 1998). Self-injury is generally a very taboo topic, because, by its very nature, it is considered socially unacceptable. Therefore, when we talk about self-injury in this book, we don't mean tattooing, body piercing, or other, similar culturally accepted behaviors. Instead, we specifically mean cutting, hitting, burning, or scratching oneself intentionally, with the purpose of harming one's body.

You will notice that in general parlance the word "cutting" is often used interchangeably with "self-injury," since many individuals will choose this as their primary method of self-injury. In the media, the term "cutting" seems to be used almost exclusively when discussing self-injury among teens. Keep in mind, however, that those who cut may also engage in other forms of self-injury.

HOW TO USE THIS BOOK

This book has been designed as a handbook for parents of children who are, or may be, self-injuring. We want to dispel the mystery that surrounds this often-misunderstood behavior, which seems to be on the rise among adolescents and young adults. We hope that you will use our book (and our years of combined knowledge and experience in helping kids and parents deal with self-injury) as a step-by-step guide to understanding, talking about, and getting help so your child may overcome self-injury. Each chapter builds on the one before it, and each is specifically designed with parents in mind, to help you think and talk about self-injury in a practical and realistic way.

We understand the anxiety that you are likely feeling if your child is hurting him- or herself. We also know that many parents hope that if they ignore self-injury, especially when it doesn't seem life threatening, their children will grow out of this very disturbing "phase." It is our hope that you will use each chapter of this book to guide you through the storm of your own painful emotions and help you establish a dialogue with your child about self-injury, so that you can stay focused on your child—instead of being distracted or hindered by your own pain, confusion, discomfort, and other feelings that may keep you from getting your child the right help.

We also want parents who read our book to learn some basic strategies that will not only help get their children into therapy but will also allow them to be supportive partners in the therapeutic process. We will teach you what to do when your child comes to you with an urge to cut, how to deal with the problems that lead to cutting, and how to validate your child's emotions without condoning unhealthy behaviors.

Most of all, we want to empower you by giving you the knowledge and insight necessary to be the best parent you can be to your self-injuring child. *We want you to talk with your child about self-injury,* armed with the right questions and the knowledge and insight to provide real answers. We want you to trust yourself to handle the very uncomfortable issue of self-injury, so your child can in turn trust *you* to act in a helpful way—reducing the drama around the behavior and effectively addressing the real emotional issues that contribute to it.

Although documented rates of self-injury are significantly higher in females, this book was written to help parents of all self-injuring children, regardless of gender, so when referring to the self-injuring child we've alternated genders throughout the book, using the feminine in one chapter and the masculine in the next. We encourage you to substitute your own child's gender when necessary.

WHAT YOU MAY BE FEELING

When an injured child comes to a parent, an array of emotions, questions, and plans of action will likely begin swirling in the parent's head. Filled with anguish, fear, and other strong feelings, parents would also inevitably want to know who or what harmed their child, the circumstances that led up to the injury, and why and how it happened. Finally, when given the answers to these questions, parents would likely snap into harm-prevention mode and would attempt to seek out and remove or destroy what they perceived to be the source of harm (whether circumstance, object, or person) to assure both themselves and their child that this would, in fact, never happen again. All of this is normal. It would be pretty ridiculous to expect yourself to approach such a situation with the emotional detachment of a Vulcan. However, we want to help you balance out your intense feelings with some cool logic, so that you can talk to your child as a concerned and educated parent, one who understands your child's pain and behavior, and who has a plan for dealing with both.

In our experience as clinicians, parents' feelings, thoughts, and reactions regarding a child's injury tend not to vary tremendously, regardless of who inflicted the injury, or the circumstances surrounding it. We have observed similar emotional reactions in many parents when they first realize that their child may be engaging in self-harm. These include the following:

- **Disbelief:** "My child's guidance counselor called and said that he thinks that she is cutting herself. Her friends apparently went to him because they're 'concerned' about her. I can't believe that she would be hurting herself on purpose. Couldn't they just be out to get her? She's such a good student and a nice girl. Why would she want to hurt herself?"

- **Denial:** "I cannot accept that my otherwise well-adjusted teen would hurt herself for no reason. Her life is fine. She must have gotten scratched by the cat. There must be some kind of mistake. There is no way she would hurt herself."

- **Anger:** "We work so hard to give her everything she wants and needs! How could she just turn around and do something like this? She knows that this is unacceptable behavior. She's acting crazy! Doesn't she know that people are going to think she's nuts?"

- **Embarrassment:** "People will think that our family is messed up because she's hurting herself. What will they think of us as parents?"

- **Fear and anxiety:** "Does this mean that she wants to kill herself? I don't know how to keep her safe and I'm so worried that something even worse may be happening."

- **Helplessness:** "This is so out of my realm of experience. I have no idea what to do. I don't think I can even talk to her about this."

- **Guilt:** "Did I make her do this to herself? Maybe I don't spend enough time with her, or maybe she's doing this because I punished her for her lousy grades."

The key thing to remember is that none of your feelings or thoughts are wrong; it's just important not to let these feelings and thoughts steer your behavioral responses when you realize that your child is engaging in self-injury.

Trying to cope with your own emotional reactions while attempting to take care of your child places both parent and child in a very difficult situation. A parent may feel angry and helpless; however, the anger may be focused on the child's behavior or even at the child, and the parent's expressions of helplessness may be perceived by the child as a sign that the parent is, in effect, powerless to help in this situation. In addition, when the parent invariably asks, "How did this happen?" "Why did you do this?" and "What would make you want to hurt yourself?" the child may not be able to explain her behavior effectively, which only adds to the pain and confusion of both parties. Also, the actions that a parent in harm-prevention mode might take, in the absence of good answers to the previous questions, might be misguided or only partially effective. At worst, these actions could cause the child to lose trust in the parent and hide evidence of future self-injury episodes, or even increase self-injury as a result of feeling misunderstood, invalidated, or alienated.

Therefore, as a parent, the better you understand self-injury, the more comfortably and confidently you will be able to discuss it with your child. The ability to address the issue of self-injury with knowledge, understanding, and confidence will inspire your child's trust and assist you in developing an effective plan to address this distressing issue. This, in and of itself, is invaluable. The more your child senses that you understand the behavior (especially if the child herself does not fully understand it) and know how to handle it, the greater your chances of establishing an open dialogue and getting your child the right kind of help. This book was developed with these specific goals in mind.

HOW YOU CAN HELP

Of course, you are reading this book because you want to know how you can help your child deal with self-injury. The first thing you can do to be helpful is to *identify your own emotional reaction* to the knowledge that your child is hurting herself. There are no wrong reactions, but not knowing or denying how you feel could get you blindsided when you try to approach your child about her self-injury. We are not telling you to stay calm and not panic. Of course you're panicked—your child is harming herself. However, remember that you want to focus on your child, not on yourself, so identifying how you feel at the outset will help you to keep your own emotions and reactions in perspective. Also, your child will probably ask you questions like "Are you mad?" so you may want to think about how to best answer these questions. For example, if you were angry at first, you might say, "Yeah, I was angry, but then I realized that you're not doing this to me; you're doing this to yourself. Now I feel more concerned about helping you out. This isn't about me and how I feel. I can handle my feelings. You seem to be the one in pain. Let's focus on you."

Once you've identified your feelings, you might realize that you're having a hard time keeping them in check. You might be stricken with panic, or you might feel really guilty. The next thing to do is to *make a plan of action that is not based only on your feelings*. Generally, when our behaviors are driven by intense emotions—that is, when we make decisions with our guts and not our heads—we may overlook some good solutions (this is part of what you will be working on with your child, so modeling it is key). For this reason, you'll find it beneficial to take some time to calm down and plan how you will approach your child, what resources you will consult, and what intervention strategy will help you to act more adaptively than your feelings alone would allow. We hope that you will use this book to help guide you in this exact process.

The next, and perhaps most important, thing you can do to help your child is to *resolve not to avoid this issue*. Your child is hurting herself. If you have to repeat it one hundred times in order to make it real, do so. Then plan not to sweep it under the rug. The more committed you are to dealing with self-injury, the more your child will deal with it too. In our experience, kids who perceive that their parents aren't consistently addressing the issue have more trouble coping. If it's not discussed, they may sense that their parents have lost interest, no longer perceive it as an important issue, or, in the worst case, don't care. Self-injury is now part of your life. It may not always be, but for the moment it is. Deal with it openly, daily, and consistently. You're not okay with the fact that your child is engaging in self-harm, but by avoiding the issue you may be sending the message that you *are* okay with it.

Finally, *involve professionals*. Even though we're professionals ourselves, we all agree that we lack the objectivity necessary to treat our own children. Therefore, please don't expect yourself to be able to deal with your child's self-injury alone. Using this book as a guide, find the right clinicians and other resources and get them on your child's team right away.

SELF-INJURY IS TREATABLE

Now that you've read the above heading, exhale and say it again to yourself: "Self-injury is treatable." What this means is that the right kind of help is just around the corner, and you can actually have some hope. We know things seem really confusing and bleak when your child is hurting, but getting connected with the right treatment professionals will allow you to breathe a little easier: you'll feel less anxious knowing that your child's issues will now be addressed, and that you will learn how to handle these issues better, too.

Cognitive behavioral therapy (CBT), which focuses on identifying and challenging faulty and rigid thinking (which can contribute to emotional distress) and on changing unhealthy or problematic behaviors (such as self-injury), holds the most promise for treating self-injury. Though supportive or insight-oriented therapies are quite useful for treating some of the underlying emotional issues in those who self-injure, they are not the treatments of choice for self-injury.

In fact, a specific type of CBT, dialectical behavior therapy (DBT), which was developed by Marsha Linehan (1993a), has been found to be effective at treating those who engage in self-injury, as well as those who are chronically suicidal. DBT focuses on helping self-injurers learn to regulate their emotions and gain interpersonal skills (which helps to reduce conflicts, and get individual needs met in an appropriate way) while also achieving the goals of more traditional CBT. The goal of DBT is to balance intense emotions with logic, in order to utilize a style of thinking and decision making that will likely lead to healthier, more adaptive behavioral choices (Linehan 1993a).

Medication management may also play a role in your child's treatment. Though we are psychologists, not psychiatrists, we acknowledge the important role that medication can play in effectively treating self-injurious behavior and the emotional disturbances that lead to it. We recommend consulting a psychiatrist to find out whether medication might help your child to deal with difficult emotions without resorting to unhealthy behaviors.

ABOUT THE AUTHORS

While working together for several years at the Bio-Behavioral Institute, a research and clinical facility dedicated to the cognitive, behavioral, and pharmacological treatment of anxiety and mood disorders in children, adolescents, and adults, we have found that we are treating adolescents engaging in self-injury in increasing numbers. We've also noted that many of them have had trouble finding help.

Dr. McVey-Noble is a cognitive behavioral psychologist who began treating self-injury during her psychology internship in an inpatient setting, working with many individuals with borderline personality disorder. She became interested in applying DBT to the treatment of self-injury in teens, because of its success in reducing and stopping self-harm behaviors in adults. She has been with the Bio-Behavioral Institute for more than five years, where she works with Dr. Khemlani-Patel and Dr. Neziroglu treating obsessive-compulsive spectrum disorders in people of all ages and developing DBT-based treatment strategies for self-injuring adolescents and their families.

Dr. Khemlani-Patel has been with the Bio-Behavioral Institute for eight years, and she uses DBT-based treatment with her self-injuring patients with much success. She has extensive experience treating body dysmorphic disorder, and it was in this patient group that she first encountered self-injurious behavior. She has found that DBT-based treatment is the most effective approach when working with self-injuring teens and their families.

Dr. Neziroglu is a cofounder of the Bio-Behavioral Institute, which is now in its twenty-seventh year. She has been a pioneer in the field of CBT and has applied cognitive behavioral therapy in the treatment of obsessive-compulsive disorder, body dysmorphic disorder, and the related disorders for three decades. In addition, she has also more recently applied CBT to the treatment of self-injury. Like her colleagues, she has observed the increasing trend toward self-injury among teens and adolescents, and together with Dr. McVey-Noble and Dr. Khemlani-Patel she is working to develop specific DBT-based treatment techniques to address these issues in adolescents.

WHY WE WROTE THIS BOOK

As psychologists, we recognize that self-injury in teens is on the rise, but we also know that it's been around for a long time and has only recently received the attention necessary to encourage self-injurers to come out of the closet. We view self-injury as both an issue in itself and a symptom of broader psychological problems. Our combined experience has taught us that, untreated, self-injurious behavior tends not to go away very easily. We see a lot of very frustrated teens and parents who have earnestly tried to find the right treatment and have been thwarted at every turn.

WHY WOULD ANYONE HURT THEMSELVES ON PURPOSE?

Self-injury seems to go against our most basic biological survival instincts—which cause us to spend a lot of time trying to take care of ourselves, to ensure our safety and longevity. The truth is, like smokers, many individuals who self-injure do not perceive their behaviors as very harmful. In fact, many individuals who self-injure report that they wear seatbelts, don't smoke, and would never consider getting into a car with someone who had been drinking. It may seem strange, but a lot of people who engage in self-injury actually state that they do it to get relief from overwhelming negative emotions. They report using self-injury to tone down intense feelings of frustration, anger, jealousy, sadness, loneliness, or being overwhelmed. Some individuals report injuring themselves when they are feeling numb or empty, in order to "feel something," as if the pain that they are inflicting on themselves serves as a reminder that they really do exist and really are alive. If this seems hard to imagine, consider the explanation given by one articulate seventeen-year-old: "All day I go to school and I act like I'm alive. I feel dead inside. It's like I'm faking it all day long until I get home. The only thing that gets me through is knowing that when that last bell rings, I'm thirty minutes away from relief. When I get home, the first thing I do is go to the bathroom and cut. It's the first time all day that I feel anything. It's such a relief that it doesn't even hurt. It almost feels like I was frozen, and when I cut I'm thawing out."

If the thought of cutting, burning, or otherwise intentionally injuring yourself makes your skin crawl, consider yourself lucky. For individuals prone to self-injury, the initial thought might be appalling, but somewhere in their minds it resonates and may gradually make more sense to them over time.

Then there are those, particularly adolescents, who don't really like self-injury but find in it a means of self-expression that is more powerful than any other they know. Maybe they injure themselves because they are struggling with painful emotions that they feel power-less to explain, because they are keeping secrets that they think they can't reveal, or because they think that they are flawed and need to be punished. What better way to express that you hate yourself or your body than by injuring it? Although some individuals who self-injure have body-image disturbances or histories of sexual abuse, many injure for a variety of other reasons, which can be as varied as the individuals themselves. Some just lack better ways to express their intense emotions or their need for attention and help. However, research suggests that individuals with histories of sexual abuse and eating disorders are significantly more likely to turn to self-injury, and at earlier ages (McKay, Kulchycky, and Danyko 2000).

We think that the link between these three behavioral disturbances is the disturbed perception of and relationship with one's body that occurs when one becomes alienated from it, as is seen in victims of sexual abuse and individuals who have significant body-image and disordered eating problems. When you think about it, it almost makes sense: if you considered your body to be the cause of all of your pain and sadness, then you too might be inclined to injure it in order to feel more in control of it.

Some children who self-injure, especially those who are very young, seem to deal with negative emotions that are so intense as to be unfathomable. How could such a little kid feel so bad? Perhaps it's the result of powerful peer pressure to look a certain way, to earn perfect grades, or to wear particular types of clothing. Some children who don't measure up (or perceive that they don't) become extremely self-critical and, again, may use self-injury as a punishment for their failure to achieve their goals.

As a parent, you might be feeling guilty for putting a little pressure on a child whose grades are lagging or who seems to be having trouble fitting in. But it's not your fault. You can't make a child cut. However, your child may indeed be struggling with self-esteem issues that go far beyond normal childhood or adolescent insecurity. If this is the case, more pressure could lead to more self-injury, so identifying the source of your child's insecurity or the reason the child thinks she doesn't measure up will be much more valuable than applying additional pressure.

Regardless of the reason someone is self-injuring, we agree that self-injury is an issue that deserves immediate attention and intervention. If it is ignored, it only tends to get worse.

IS SELF-INJURY JUST A WAY TO TRY TO GET ATTENTION?

The answer to this question is yes—and no. The self-harming person might want to display the results of the behavior to show exactly how much pain she is in, or she might try to keep it quiet, just another in a cache of what she perceives to be her "dirty little secrets."

Some people who self-injure do so in conspicuous places on their bodies, like wrists or forearms, or more rarely on their faces; however, others are more likely to self-injure in places that can easily be hidden, such as on the ankles, hips, or chest. Those who broadcast it want you to know that they are struggling (though they might still resist attempts at intervention), while those who keep their self-injuries hidden are more likely to want to conceal their pain.

In either case, once you have discovered that your child is injuring herself, pay attention to it. Many parents report initially accepting their children's lame excuses for their injuries ("The cat scratched me" or "I got cut when I fell into a bush") because of their own discomfort with the topic. However, it's likely that your child is even more uncomfortable than you are if she has resorted to this behavior as a way to cope. Please don't send the message that you're too uncomfortable with the subject to get your child the medical and psychological attention she needs, even if she tries to resist it.

Self-injury deserves attention, and so does your child. Due to the fact that self-injury is a socially unacceptable behavior, it tends to put others off. Try hard not to react to your own emotions around your child's injuries, and remember that self-injury is a sign that your child is struggling with something so serious that it is threatening her safety and potentially her life. You should certainly acknowledge your own feelings, but let your behaviors be driven by what you logically know your child needs you to do.

Several years ago, we met a family embroiled in a bitter divorce. Both parents were so focused on their own anger at each other and guilt about their daughter's self-injury that they had delayed seeking treatment for her. When we got the initial call, her father was tearful, guilty, and so traumatized that he actually thought that we would blame him and recommend that he not have contact with his child. The opposite was true, actually—we recommended that he be present at her consultation. During our meeting, the teenager herself was able to articulate to her parents that she blamed neither of them but had become very frustrated about their fighting, because she felt that it was causing them to ignore her issues. The more we focused on her feelings and needs (and less on her parents), the better she got. In fact, the one thing her parents were able to agree on was their unconditional love for their daughter and their firm commitment to her treatment.

BY RESPONDING TO THIS BEHAVIOR, COULDN'T I JUST BE FEEDING INTO IT?

Yes, you could, or you might actually be helping your child gain the control she needs to stop self-injuring. Remember, self-injury isn't only about hurting oneself. It's usually driven by other problems that very likely require your attention. It's the kind of attention and response you provide that counts.

Certain parental reactions are generally more likely to feed into and increase the self-injury. For example, if your child is injuring in response to excessive conflict or feelings of inadequacy, and you react with extreme anger and punishment, then this might actually increase or escalate the problem. If your child's self-injury is attention seeking, and you choose to ignore it because of your own discomfort, then the behavior may also escalate until ignoring is no longer an option.

Similarly, the level of intensity of the parental response may also contribute to an increase or reduction in the child's self-injury. A parent who over-responds to a child's self-injury, making the injuries the focus of attention rather than dealing with the underlying causes of the behavior, may wind up inadvertently reinforcing it and increasing the likelihood of repetition. Similarly, a parent who under-responds to the discovery, or the revelation, of a child's self-injury runs the risk of tacitly condoning such behavior as a coping mechanism. In this case also, the self-injury is likely to continue and may even escalate.

In addition, a result of both over- and under-responding to self-injury is that the parent doesn't help the child explore the triggers for self-injury and in effect does not help the child gain insight into the problems that likely led up to the injury. When we are working with families in therapy, we spend a lot of time helping both adolescents and parents to identify the antecedents to self-injury, whether emotional, interpersonal, or situational. This may include beliefs about self-injury (for example, "My child is just doing it for attention" or "If I cut even once, I've ruined everything, and my parents will be angry, so I have no reason to stop") and the consequences of self-injury (emotional, social, physical, and so on). Basically, we ask, "What match set off this explosion, and what is its fuel source?"

When a parent is able to view the injury as an end result of other problems that the child is experiencing, and when the parent can help the child identify these problems in relation to the pattern of self-injury, that parent will begin to erode links in the chain of self-injurious behavior. In this case, the parent's appropriate questions and attention do not reinforce the behavior by making it the focus of their concern, or by dismissing it as "not that bad." Instead, the questions and attention will help the child feel understood and may actually give the child the tools to understand his or her own self-injurious behavior.

COULDN'T THIS BE JUST A PASSING PHASE?

Sure, it could. But are you really willing to take that risk?

We find that the longer one waits to get help for a loved one who is self-injuring, the harder self-injury becomes to treat. In essence, self-injury is addictive. It may seem hard to believe, but when individuals with the biological predisposition to self-injure actually engage in that behavior, they report a sense of relief, increased calm, and even elation. Why? Theoretically, the brain of someone with a predisposition to self-injure reacts to self-injury by releasing opioids, or pleasure chemicals, which result in a sense of increased well-being (Favazza 1998). The problem with this reaction is that an area of the brain referred to as the "reward circuit," or the "pleasure center," is activated in this process. It is hypothesized that this is the area of the brain that is involved in addiction, and, as with other addictive behaviors, repetition and escalation become necessary in order to produce the same results. Some research suggests that by about the thirtieth cut, an individual may already be hooked, resulting in an addiction-like behavior that is unlikely to go away on its own (Fauazza 1998).

It seems that some people's brains are hardwired to feel soothed by cutting and experience it as a rapid and pleasurable discharge of intense negative emotion. Almost all of the teens we work with express that they "crave" self-injury when they are trying to stop. They use terms like "cut junkie," "addict," and "hooked" to describe themselves and their dependence on self-injury as a coping strategy. Often, these adolescents express that when they are making a conscious effort to stop injuring themselves, they are irritable, moody, and short tempered. One young woman who had given up cigarettes before she gave up self-injury stated that "quitting smoking was easier than quitting cutting."

In individuals who are not predisposed to find self-injury so pleasing, it may indeed just be a passing phase, an attempt to get relief, a cry for help, a way to punish themselves for a perceived weakness or wrongdoing, or a way to express negative emotions that they can't explain. However, for the individuals mentioned above, self-injury becomes like a drug habit that they feel powerless to break. Even we clinicians can't always be sure which scenario we're dealing with, so we treat all of our patients who self-injure as if they have the potential to get hooked on their behaviors. We encourage parents to do the same.

WHY IS IT IMPORTANT TO GET HELP?

First, as you are already aware, the sooner you find help and stop your child's self-injury cycle, the easier treatment will be for your child. We know that when people wait until the problem of self-injury is just too big to ignore, it is actually harder to treat, for a few reasons:

- It has become almost addictive.

- It has become a highly reinforcing way to find relief from negative emotions.

- It may be getting a lot of the wrong type of attention.

- It has become a well-practiced, automatic response to stress.

Therefore, the quicker you deal with the problem and get the appropriate help, the less your child will have to struggle to break extremely difficult behavioral patterns, and the more likely it is that her other issues will be addressed. Arresting self-injury as early as possible leads to fewer long-term complications, both medical and psychological.

In addition, even though you will likely be highly qualified to deal with your adolescent's self-injury in a parental capacity after reading this book, you still won't be capable of acting as your child's therapist or psychiatrist. Expecting yourself to act in this capacity would very likely be unhealthy for you and for your child. Your child needs you to be her parent, no more and no less. When parents try to control their children's treatment, children feel as if they have gained doctors but lost their parents. Your role as a parent—to accept, guide, support, protect, and, most of all, love your child (whether or not you like or accept her behavior)—is totally unique. No treatment professional on the planet could ever fill your shoes.

Additionally, the emotional strain of trying to come up with all the answers for your child, even if you were a mental health professional with specific training, would be tremendous. The fact that this child is yours immediately affects your objectivity and perspective. And that is why we recommend utilizing highly trained treatment professionals instead of trying to do it all yourself. They will not try to parent your child (although they may give advice on how to do so), because they understand that they could never fill your shoes. Keep two roles separate and defined is best for you, your child treatment, and the parent-child relationship.

Getting help from a professional is important for several reasons:

- It lets your child know that you take her self-injury and the precipitating problems seriously.

- It allows a trained professional to evaluate for other issues—such as depression and related mood disturbances, suicidality, eating disorders and other body-image problems, sexual abuse, anxiety disorders, and substance abuse—that might be contributing to your child's self-injury.

- It provides structure and a framework for how these issues will be dealt with (which will in turn reduce your anxiety along with your child's).

- The right treatment professionals will have specific, well-researched diagnostic tools and therapeutic techniques and/or pharmacological interventions at their disposal.

- Your child will have another resource to work with and may actually disclose more to the professionals, since she will be less concerned with hurting your feelings or damaging your relationship.

- You will be able to focus more on your bond with your child, and less on what is "wrong" in this situation.

In our clinical practice, we have noticed that when families come in for help with dealing with their adolescents' self-injury, the minute a comprehensive plan is presented, all parties involved begin to relax. Even if the plan involves suicide assessment, medical intervention, or even (in severe cases) hospitalization, the organizational structure provided by the treatment professional or team seems to lead to immediate tension reduction for both parents and children.

The sooner treatment is initiated, the sooner your child will be on the road to health. Focused treatment helps. It may take time, and it may require resources that aren't easy to gather, but once you have a plan in place that involves a comprehensive treatment team (made up of parents, child, psychologist, psychiatrist, and school personnel, for example) you will be closer to your goal. We really don't think of anyone as "beyond help"; rather, we prefer to think of those who haven't yet found relief as not having had enough help, or the right kind of help. Have confidence that if you are dealing effectively with your child's self-injury, the behavior will stop.

WHAT KIND OF HELP IS BEST?

Though there are many community resources, such as school personnel, clergy, other parents, and crisis hotlines, that can provide you and your adolescent with tremendous support during times of stress or turmoil, when you are dealing with your child's tendency toward self-injury, we recommend seeking out specifically trained treatment personnel. All of the above-mentioned resources can be helpful, but only someone with the specific training to treat self-injury and its related issues will be qualified to really help your child.

Just because an individual is a psychiatrist (a medical doctor who is trained to prescribe the appropriate medications) or a psychologist (a professional who is trained to provide therapy but does not prescribe medication), this does not mean that he or she is immediately qualified to treat your child. When seeking out such a treatment professional, inquire whether the person treats adolescents, whether and how often he or she has dealt with self-injury, and what his or her therapeutic orientation is.

If the individual doesn't have specific training to treat children and/or adolescents, has only occasionally seen patients with self-injurious tendencies, or does not have a cognitive behavioral orientation (this concept will be explained further in the section on how to select a therapist), then this is probably not the best treatment professional for your child. Be selective in choosing your treatment professionals, and do ask these important questions even if you feel uncomfortable. A well-trained professional will only respect you for trying to find the best resources for your child.

In addition, keep in mind that different types of professionals will have different services to offer. Your child might need a few different professionals on her team. For example, if your child has an eating disorder in addition to self-injury, then she will likely need to see a psychologist (for therapy), a psychiatrist (for medication), a nutritionist (for dietary intervention), and possibly a physician (for medical monitoring). However, treatment is not always this complicated, and many adolescents can be served very well by a psychologist, or a psychologist and psychiatrist who work as a team.

Whatever the level of care that you seek, if you or your child does not feel that her problems are being comprehensively addressed by your current treatment professional(s), do not be afraid to seek out other resources. The longer self-injury goes untreated or undertreated, the harder it is on everyone involved.

1

Self-Injury: Just the Facts

In order to help your child, it is important that you be armed with the proper knowledge about self-injury. In this chapter you will learn all the basic information about self-injury, including the categories and methods of self-injury and some possible reasons why your child might be engaging in the behavior. In this chapter, we will be addressing parents' most common questions regarding self-injury.

Before we go any further, you may want to complete the screening questionnaire below, which we have developed to help you identify whether your child is actually engaging in self-injury. Although answering yes to any of these questions alone may not signal that a problem currently exists, positive responses to several of these could indicate that your child is at risk. Other issues, such as substance abuse, depression, or eating disorders, can also elevate your child's score. Use this questionnaire only as an initial screening instrument, followed by a proper evaluation by a qualified mental health professional.

SELF-INJURY SCREENING QUESTIONNAIRE

1. Has your child recently demonstrated a change in his behavior (eating, sleeping, school performance, level of socialization, appearance)?

2. Has your child recently demonstrated a dramatic change in mood (hostile, angry, sad, or tearful)?

3. Has your child recently demonstrated erratic mood changes from one moment or day to the next?

4. Has your child been more secretive than usual?

5. Has your child been spending more time alone or with a different group of friends?

6. Has your child been wearing different clothes or jewelry that might camouflage scars or injuries, such as long sleeves, cuff bracelets, turtlenecks, or long pants in hot weather?

7. Has your child been wearing more adhesive or gauze bandages lately, or have you noticed missing medical supplies from your medicine cabinet or first-aid kit?

8. Does your child talk about self-injury (perhaps mentioning friends who self-injure, asking whether you have ever self-injured, or threatening self-injury)?

9. Have you seen more cuts or scratches on your child than usual?

10. Has your child suddenly begun avoiding sports or other activities (such as dance, swimming, or martial arts) that would require others to see more of his body or be in close physical contact?

11. Is your child refusing to go for his yearly doctor's appointment?

12. Have you noticed your child carrying around implements that could be used for self-harm, such as paper clips, scissors, razors, safety pins, tweezers, and/or knives?

13. Does your child make excuses for unexplained scratches, bruises, or marks on his body (such as "The cat scratched me," "I fell into a bush," or "I was holding a glass and it broke")?

14. Does your child seem to be in frequent conflict with his friends?

15. Does your child seem to be withdrawing from things that he previously enjoyed?

16. Do any of your child's friends engage in self-injury?

17. Have your child's friends, other family members, or school personnel expressed concern about your child or his safety?

18. Has your child spoken about suicide?

19. Has your child's appearance changed dramatically (such as a sudden increase or decrease in body weight, or a drastic change in your child's mode of dress)?

20. Has your child been sexually abused?

If you answered yes to more than two of the above questions, we strongly suggest seeking the advice of a trained mental health professional. This does not always mean that a child is self-injuring, but it can suggest that he may be in some type of distress and that consultation with a professional is warranted.

WHAT ARE THE TYPES OF SELF-INJURY?

The term "self-injury" can refer to a wide variety of behaviors under a wide variety of circumstances. Before we can proceed further, it is important for you to know what types of injury exist and which ones we will be covering in this book. The types of self-injury have been organized into four major categories by a well-known researcher, Armando Favazza (1998). These categories have helped researchers and clinicians understand each patient's behavior and decide on the treatment that best fits the problem.

This book will focus on *impulsive self-injury*—direct, intentional, repetitive behavior that can result in mild to moderate physical injury (Suyemoto 1998), such as cutting, burning, hitting, picking, and puncturing. Before we cover all the aspects of this type of self-injury in detail, we would like to briefly introduce you to the other forms of self-injury, which we will not be focusing on in this book.

The term *major self-injury* refers to dramatic acts, such as amputating one's own limbs, gouging out one's eyes, or self-castration. This type of self-injury is quite rare and tends to be a single and sudden isolated event. This occurs most often when the person is not in touch with reality, such as during a psychotic, manic, or drug-induced episode. The result of this type of self-injury is usually quite severe and life threatening. Major self-injury differs from impulsive self-injury in many ways, not only in the degree of damage done to the body but also in the psychological state of the individual; impulsive self-injury does not occur as a direct result of a psychosis, mania, or drug intoxication.

Stereotypic self-injury refers to repetitive, monotonous, self-stimulating behaviors, such as head banging, skin picking, self-biting, and self-hitting. Although the behaviors themselves overlap with impulsive self-injury, the cause and intention of the behavior is quite different. This type of self-injury is associated with specific syndromes diagnosed in infancy or childhood, such as mental retardation, autism, Lesch-Nyhan syndrome, and Prader-Willi syndrome and may be seen in patients in institutionalized settings. With this type of self-injury, the person often doesn't have a clear psychological reason why they are engaging in self-injury; it is sometimes a biological drive without particular emotional meaning. Impulsive self-injury, on the other hand, tends to be psychologically and biologically motivated—a means to cope with emotional pain.

Compulsive self-injury is usually associated with the obsessive-compulsive spectrum disorders, which are characterized by repetitive intrusive thoughts and/or repetitive compulsive behaviors. Compulsive self-injury is seen in people with Tourette's syndrome, trichotillomania, and body dysmorphic disorder. Typically, these behaviors include hair pulling, skin picking, and nail biting. Often they are repetitive, habit-driven behaviors that may or may not be under the person's conscious control. We all know individuals who constantly bite their nails, pick their cuticles, or pick at superficial scratches or mosquito bites. These behaviors tend to be habits and are only considered to be disorders if they interfere with the person's ability to participate in life on a daily basis. These habitual behaviors may occur on their own, but they are also commonly seen in people already diagnosed with trichotillomania, or compulsive hair pulling. In the case of body dysmorphic disorder, which involves an intense preoccupation with one's physical appearance, the compulsive self-injury is done in order to correct or improve one's appearance. Typically, the person is concerned with their skin and will pick or dig at acne or blemishes in an attempt to "fix" the problem.

From this point forward, when we use the term "self-injury," we will be referring strictly to behaviors that fall under the "impulsive" category: self-injury that is done purposefully and is intended to reduce emotional distress or pain.

WHO ENGAGES IN SELF-INJURY?

The typical self-injurer is female. This is not to say that there are no males who engage in self-injury. However, there are twice as many females as males who report self-injurious behavior (although we think that this number may be low, because males may underreport this symptom in treatment or psychiatric settings, viewing it as a behavior more commonly associated with females).

Generally, the first episode of self-injury occurs between the ages of fourteen and sixteen. Self-injury is not just a teen phenomenon, however. For many individuals, the behavior may begin in adolescence but can persist well into adulthood. Some studies suggest that self-injury may still be present in women even into their forties and fifties (Sansone, Gaither, and Songer 2002).

The prevalence rates within the population vary depending upon the setting being studied. In the general population, self-injury is estimated to occur in 1 to 4 percent of individuals (Briere and Gil 1998; Favazza and Conterio 1989). But in a typical high school setting, an alarming 14 percent of students reported having engaged in self-injury at some point in time (Ross and Heath 2002). This means that in a typical suburban American high school of 1,000 students, 140 students may be self-injurers. Similar rates were estimated, at approximately 12 percent, in a college sample (Favazza 1998).

As one would surmise, rates of self-injury are higher in individuals who already demonstrate psychological or psychiatric issues. In general, approximately 20 percent of individuals seeking psychiatric or psychological services report engaging in self-injury (Briere and Gil 1998). Studies have found that 40 to 60 percent of adolescents hospitalized in psychiatric settings report actively engaging in self-injurious behavior (DiClemente, Ponton, and Hartley 1991).

Recently, educators around the country have been attempting to address the issue in their schools by seeking training to identify the warning signs and implement peer counseling outreach programs. Teen magazines have also begun to run articles on self-injury. A variety of adolescent-oriented Web sites focus on the topic, and even popular media icons like Angelina Jolie, Winona Ryder, and Johnny Depp have come forward to admit that at one time they engaged in self-injury. Though this behavior has likely been present throughout the ages, it is clearly occurring in adolescents at a higher frequency than most parents are comfortable with. Self-injury is a behavior that seems to be on the rise and that requires clinical attention.

■ Jane's Story

We saw Jane when she was twenty and about to change colleges. Her parents were concerned about a psychiatrist's recommendation that she be placed on antidepressants for depression. The parents did not see her as depressed, but they were nevertheless upset by her poor eating habits and perfectionism. They also reported that approximately seven years before, while at camp, Jane had written some stories discussing cutting behavior. Jane shared her stories with several other campers and, feeling concerned, the camp officials contacted her parents. When they questioned Jane about the stories, she told them that she wasn't doing it, but that other kids were and she was just wondering what it would feel like. They believed her and never pursued it further. Several years later, however, Jane confessed to them that she had started cutting in camp, along with engaging in some disturbed eating behavior, and continued after she returned home. In fact, at the time she came to see us she had just recently stopped cutting but was finding it difficult to resist the urge. During our cognitive behavioral therapy sessions it became clear that Jane was numb. She felt good only on the days when she did not eat at all (though this is not direct self-injury, it is a dangerous behavior that can serve the same purpose as cutting). During the next few months, we taught her how to express her feelings directly without engaging in dangerous, self-destructive behaviors.

WHAT ARE THE COMMON METHODS OF SELF-INJURY?

Theoretically, there may be an endless variety of methods of self-injury. However, a number of studies suggest that cutting tends to be the most common method (Favazza 1998). Other types of self-injury include self-hitting, pinching, scratching, biting, burning, punching, head banging, puncturing, skin picking, and interfering with wound healing (the latter involves picking at a preexisting scar or scab, such as a scratch or mosquito bite, until it bleeds, or reopening a wound from a prior occurrence of self-injury). One study of 440 adolescents found that the majority only engaged in one method of self-injury, which means that your child may have a favored method, such as cutting or burning (Ross and Heath 2002). However, as the behavior tends to escalate, it is not uncommon for a self-injurer to try other methods of injury as well.

WHAT IMPLEMENTS IS MY CHILD USING TO SELF-INJURE?

Almost any implement can be used to cause harm, including razor blades, knives, and scissors. In some cases, one particular tool is preferred for self-injuring, but in our clinical practice we have also seen patients seek out the closest implement available to them, such as a piece of broken glass, a paper clip, a nail clipper, or even a pen cap. In these circumstances, the behavior is more impulsive rather than planned.

If your child is self-injuring frequently, it is quite likely that he is carrying his tool(s) around with him on a regular basis. Many parents think that removing the child's implements of choice will prevent the child from hurting himself. However, if an individual is bent on self-injury, removing the tools will not solve the problem. Technically, if the urge to self-injure is strong enough, desperation can lead an emotionally distraught self-injurer to turn anything from a spiral binder to a broken CD case into a weapon.

Though the act of self-injury may seem totally irrational and impulsive, a number of our patients over the years have reported sterilizing their injury tools with heat or isopropyl alcohol. Patients have also told us that they care for their wounds, using hydrogen peroxide and topical antibiotic ointments to disinfect them, and covering them with bandages or dressings to protect them. Sometimes, this process becomes a ritual involving preparation for the injury, the act of injury, and then wound care.

It is for this reason that we caution parents to take stock of their medicine chests or first-aid kits. If the child is engaging in such a medical preparation ritual, parents will notice the aforementioned items diminishing in quantity from medicine chests; alternatively, the self-injurer might have put together a medical kit that he keeps either with him or in the area that he has chosen as a safe place to engage in self-injury.

WHERE ON HIS BODY DOES MY CHILD SELF-INJURE?

The location of the body can vary, but typically the injury is done on the arms, legs, chest, hips, scalp, abdomen, genitals, and ankles. It is important for parents to recognize that the location and type of injury can indicate the degree of risk for accidental death. An individual who is using a sharp knife and cutting quite deeply on the wrists or abdomen has a higher risk of unintentionally causing a severe or life-threatening injury during an episode of cutting. This is not to say that there are any safe body parts on which to cut, or that any act of self-injury, no matter how seemingly superficial, should go unrecognized. The fact of the matter is, however, that when an individual is cutting frequently enough, he may run out of less risky places to cut, or the behavior might escalate so that he seeks out more risky body parts in order to generate increased stimulation and relief.

HOW OFTEN DOES MY CHILD SELF-INJURE?

How often your child engages in self-injury can vary from once a year to once a month to more than once a day. One community sample of urban and suburban adolescents found that 13 percent of students who self-injured said they did so more than once a day, 28 percent reported that they injured a couple of times a week, and 20 percent said they did so a couple of times a month (Ross and Heath 2002). The remainder reported either a single episode, or infrequent self-injury. For some adolescents, the behavior is temporary and occurs during a time when they're experiencing a specific life stressor, while for others it becomes a longer-term activity. Favazza (1998) distinguishes between two types of self-injurers: repetitive and episodic. For those who engage in repeated acts of self-injury, their behaviors seem to occur in response to numerous emotional or environmental triggers. Episodic self-injurers, on the other hand, have discrete episodes of cutting only during a limited number of times in their lives. Life stressors, such as starting college or ending a romantic relationship, can trigger episodic cutting. As we will review later, the behavior can become biologically addictive quite quickly, but other factors, such as life history and mental illness, can increase the risk for the behavior to develop into a pattern.

WHAT DOES IT FEEL LIKE TO SELF-INJURE?

Parents often wonder how their children could engage in a behavior that seems so painful. However, a portion of individuals who self-injure actually report that they do not feel any pain during the behavior, instead feeling marked anesthesia, or a state of total psychological and physical disconnectedness, until after the injury has occurred. A number of our patients have reported that they experience such intense psychological pain in their daily lives that the only way to get any relief (if only temporarily) is to numb themselves by cutting. Statements such as "Cutting is like an out-of-body experience" and "It's like a drug, like a painkiller" suggest precisely this motivation.

Conversely, some individuals may actually self-injure in response to dissociation, in order to end the overwhelming numbness that grips them. Some of our patients have made statements like "I cut because I'm so numb I need to feel something" and "Sometimes, I feel like I'm nowhere, that I don't exist. When I cut, and see the blood, then feel it running down my arm, it reminds me that I'm alive, that I'm here." Though this is probably difficult to comprehend and uncomfortable for you to read, for an individual who walks around feeling completely alienated from the world, his peers, and even his own body, self-injury is an act that snaps him back into a fully connected mode. But whether cutting is done to end numbness or dissociation, or to induce numbness as an escape from pain, it is an extremely dangerous practice. The individual's impaired ability to accurately judge the intensity of his own pain puts him at greater risk of more severe cutting, or even mortal injury.

Contributing to the experience of pain or numbness during the act of self-injury is the urge that precedes it. Some individuals who self-injure describe the urge to harm themselves as being so powerful that they are unable to resist. Sometimes they are able to forestall the urge until they can reach their preferred tool and location to cut, but this is not always the case. Some of our other patients report that they feel powerless to delay the behavior and may seek out any method and location possible, finding a stall in a public restroom and using any tool they can find. Again, the more impulsive the act of injury becomes, the greater the risk to the injurer.

WHY DOES MY CHILD SELF-INJURE?

This is perhaps the most perplexing question that we can answer for you. Why is your child deliberately causing harm to his body—harm that can result in visible and sometimes permanent scars? Why is your child seeking to hurt himself further when he is probably already experiencing so much mental pain? We hope to answer this question throughout this book, beginning with the discussion below.

In order to answer this question, you may want to first learn what *function* self-injury serves in your child's life. What does it actually *do* for your child? Does cutting himself help with social isolation, improve the ability to cope with interpersonal conflict, regulate painful emotions, communicate internal anguish, and/or assist in escaping traumatic memories of abuse? In general, as behavioral therapists, we conceptualize self-injury as an unhealthy way of coping with either uncomfortable emotions or difficult life situations—feelings and situations for which your child lacks the necessary and effective coping skills. The following is a discussion of the most common reasons why your child may be self-injuring. The reasons can differ from one circumstance to another, but most self-injurers engage in the behavior for the same few reasons.

Self-Injury as a Coping Mechanism

The self-injury may provide a way for your child to regulate painful or intolerable emotions, or to express emotions that are difficult to articulate in any other way. Our patients have often said to us, "It's the only way I know how to cope" or "If I give up cutting, I'll go crazy." Often, it is even difficult for these children to identify the exact emotion they are feeling; they just know that they are in an intense amount of psychological pain. If you yourself possess the skills to cope with difficult emotions, it may seem unreasonable that your child self-injures in response to slightly challenging feelings. But the thing to remember is that your child either lacks the skill set, or the confidence to use it, in order to deal with his emotions in any other way.

The emotions that precede or trigger self-injury can be as diverse as the individuals who experience them. However, the following feelings seem to be some of the more common emotional antecedents to self-injury: anger, self-loathing, guilt, depression, frustration, loneliness, isolation, obsessionality, overstimulation, anxiety, irritability, jealousy, and numbness or dissociation.

Primarily, we view self-injury as an attempt to regulate painful emotions. Most of our patients report that their self-injury really does serve that purpose well (albeit at a very high cost: individuals who self-injure report the need for escalated acts of injury to achieve the same level of emotional relief over time). The concept of self-injury as an emotion-regulating behavior is pivotal, however, because emotional dysregulation, which is similar to disequilibrium, is a component of several different psychological disorders associated with self-injury.

Adolescents who engage in self-injury are usually unsuccessful at dealing with some combination of the negative emotions listed above. At some point, they tried self-injury as a way to cope with them. If they have self-injured more than one time, behavioral principles suggest that not only did self-injury relieve some of the negative emotions but it likely also helped them to feel calmer, more clearheaded, and more in control. In other words, self-injury is often the most potent method these children have to soothe themselves.

Let's disregard the behavior for a moment. Wouldn't we all be likely to repeat actions that led to a feeling of relief from emotional tension and instilled a sense of subjective well-being? Now, consider the behavior of self-injury. We think that almost everyone can relate to engaging in some form of self-defeating or maladaptive behavior in order to relieve emotional tension and to "make us feel better" (such as overeating, smoking, drinking to excess, avoiding necessary tasks, and giving in to others' unreasonable demands). Self-injury may be just a more direct expression of these maladaptive behaviors.

Self-Injury as a Response to the Immediate Environment

Self-injury may be viewed as a method of gaining control over not only one's emotions but also one's immediate environment. Self-injury is shocking and disturbing, so people tend to respond to it with intense emotional reactions that range from concern and nurturing to repulsion and avoidance. Thus, the behavior can be used as a way to seek help and/or attention from others or to communicate something important to a particular person.

Hence, self-injury can be effective in the following ways:

- As a cry for help or a plea asking for attention to be paid to the person's suffering; to *show* how much pain the person is experiencing even if he can't articulate it

- To communicate interpersonal boundaries ("Stay away from me; I'm dangerous" or "Get closer to me; I need help")

- To test others' devotion ("Will you still love and care for me even if I'm doing this to myself?" or "Will you save me?")

- To punish oneself or a loved one ("I'm punishing myself because I'm bad or unlovable" or "I'm punishing you because you hurt or angered me.")

HOW DID MY CHILD LEARN TO DO THIS?

Parents often wonder how their child came up with the idea to self-injure in the first place. As part of our initial evaluation, we are just as interested in the answer to that particular question. Some of our patients report having no idea how they decided to engage in the behavior, while others say they heard about it through their peers or the media. Although there have been a number of television shows and movies that have attempted to cover the topic, we certainly can't blame Hollywood for a behavior that has existed for thousands of years in many cultures around the world. We encourage parents not to focus too much on where or from whom their child might have learned self-injurious behavior. Playing the blame game certainly diverts valuable time and energy away from helping your child to stop hurting himself.

SELF-INJURY VS. SUICIDE

One of the most painful questions that a parent has to consider after learning that his or her child is self-injuring is whether the child is at risk of committing suicide. The key to answering the question is to assess the motivation behind the behavior. In other words, what is the intention of the behavior? Is the behavior done in response to painful emotions, for example, or is it intended to be a suicidal act? *Parasuicidal* behavior is any act that is nonfatal but results in tissue damage, illness, or risk of death. *Suicidal* behavior, on the other hand, is motivated by a clear intention to die. That means that an individual can use a knife to cut his arms in response to being rejected by his girlfriend versus cutting his arms in order to bleed to death. The problem is that it is sometimes difficult to distinguish between parasuicidal and suicidal behavior, because an individual can engage in both behaviors. Research indicates that approximately 50 to 90 percent of individuals who self-injure also engage in suicidal behavior (Favazza and Conterio 1989; Simeon, Stanley, and Frances 1992). Approximately 28 to 41 percent of those who self-injure may experience suicidal thoughts during an episode of self-injury (Gardner and Gardner 1975; Pattison and Kahan 1983).

As a parent, it is overwhelming to learn that your child is self-injuring, but it can be even more devastating to realize that your child may accidentally or intentionally inflict a potentially life-threatening injury. The best course of action is to immediately seek the guidance and treatment of a caring and well-trained professional who can properly assess and monitor your child's risk for suicide.

We understand that dealing with a child who is self-injuring is an extremely frustrating and anxiety-provoking situation for any parent. Living with the constant uncertainty that your child may one day die or be severely injured as a result of his own behavior is unimaginably painful and frightening. However, we ask you not to become immobilized in the face of this realization.

Consider the following: If a child drinks and drives, gets into a car with someone who has been drinking, uses drugs, or has unprotected sex, that child could also die or be severely injured as a result of his own actions—the consequences could be the same as the consequences of self-injuring. Somehow, however, it is easier to ignore the dangers that come with risky situations like drinking and driving, because they're not as disturbing as self-injury. But in the case of a child who is self-injuring, you may actually have more control and a better chance of helping him to safety than parents in the other, more ordinary-sounding situations. By offering you this book, we hope to empower you so that you are able to deal more effectively with your child's behavior and help him recover.

2

Mind and Body: The Psychological and Biological Bases of Self-Injury

Self-injury is seen in a range of psychological and psychiatric disorders, which stem from a combination of psychological, social, and biological factors. In this chapter we will explain how these variables contribute to self-injury.

PSYCHOLOGICAL BASES OF SELF-INJURY

Self-injury can occur as a symptom within a psychiatric disorder or as a behavior in itself. Our current diagnostic system, the *Diagnostic and Statistical Manual of Mental Disorders* (DSM-IV; American Psychiatric Association 1994), provides mental health professionals with the information necessary to diagnose all mental disorders based on a set of specific symptoms. It is interesting to note that the type of self-injury we are covering in this book only appears as a criterion for one particular diagnosis, borderline personality disorder (BPD), even though self-injury can actually occur within many other disorders. Besides BPD, self-injury is associated with eating disorders, dissociative disorders, and post-traumatic stress disorder (particularly when the trauma is the result of sexual abuse). We will introduce you to all of the above illnesses in which self-injury may occur. We know that as a parent you would like an explanation for why your child is harming herself. We advise you to be cautious about labeling your child as having any of the following disorders. Many of the symptoms can overlap and it takes an in-depth clinical evaluation with a trained professional to discern what may be the cause of your child's behavior.

Conditions in Which Self-Injury Occurs

Now we'll look at the various psychological disorders that may include self-injury as a symptom. In some, such as borderline personality disorder, self-injury is a more central feature of the disorder, while in others, such as major depression, self-injury may occur less frequently. We think it's important to understand the causes and correlates of self-injury well, because it may present a little differently when it is associated with particular disorders (for example, it presents in younger children when it is associated with sexual abuse and tends to be more impulsive and dangerous in the context of bipolar disorder) and may warrant slightly different treatment as a result (medications to stabilize mood are essential in treating bipolar disorder, for example).

BORDERLINE PERSONALITY DISORDER

Borderline personality disorder is usually characterized by a long-standing pattern of unstable and intense relationships, dramatic mood fluctuations, unstable self-image, feelings of emptiness, intense anger, suicidal gestures or threats, self-injurious behavior, paranoia, or dissociation during extreme stress, as well as a fear of abandonment or being alone. Individuals with BPD have extreme difficulty regulating their emotions, resulting in chaotic lives and a lack of stable, healthy relationships and stable life history. The fluctuation in emotions can be quite quick or dramatic in an individual with BPD. Parents and friends are often frustrated and genuinely confused by the individual's "sudden" shift in emotion and behavior. Family members often tell us that their loved one seems fine one moment and is crying uncontrollably the next. Individuals with BPD can experience frequent episodes of suicidality; in fact, statistics demonstrate that approximately 9 percent of individuals with this diagnosis will successfully kill themselves (Linehan 1993a). Recent research indicates that this difficulty regulating mood, due in part to the increased sensitivity in people with BPD, is biological in nature, partly involving the emotion center of the brain, called the "limbic system." In an attempt to regulate their mood, individuals with BPD often act impulsively, sometimes engaging in high-risk behaviors such as substance abuse, unsafe sex, and self-injury.

All teenagers may exhibit some of these symptoms at one time or another, especially during a crisis or life change, such as a breakup with a boyfriend or when beginning high school or college. The turmoil in adolescence can often mimic many of the symptoms of BPD, but clinicians diagnose the illness only if the pattern of behavior is longstanding (determined through a thorough evaluation).

Self-injury in BPD is more thoroughly researched than self-injury which occurs in the context of other disorders. Since a high percentage of individuals with BPD (66 to 75 percent) also have a history of abuse, the self-injury can often be associated with the trauma. In this case, the injury may provide a powerful way to cope with the flashbacks and intense memories of the abuse as well as regain control of the body. (See "Post-Traumatic Stress Disorder," below, for more on the association between trauma and self-injury.) Like other people who self-injure, individuals with BPD can also injure as a cry for help, as an emotion regulation strategy, to cope with feelings of emptiness, as a way of controlling others close to them, and as a way of communicating internal mental anguish.

EATING DISORDERS

Anorexia nervosa and bulimia are the two most recognized eating disorders. Anorexia nervosa involves a refusal to maintain a healthy body weight through weight loss methods such as severely restricting food intake and/or using laxatives and excessive exercise. Individuals with anorexia nervosa have distorted body images and see themselves as overweight despite being significantly underweight. Individuals with anorexia are usually noticeably thin and may require hospitalization for the numerous medical complications that occur with starvation.

Bulimia nervosa is characterized by ingesting an enormous amount of food in a short period of time, called "bingeing," followed by an attempt to rid the body of unwanted calories by vomiting, or "purging." Like individuals with anorexia, people with bulimia may also abuse laxatives, diuretics, and diet pills.

Both of these disorders can also involve self-injury, probably due to the intense hatred and shame that affected individuals feel toward their bodies; individuals with eating disorders may self-injure as a way to punish the body. As we mentioned earlier, another connection between eating disorders and self-injury may be due to a third variable: a history of sexual abuse. A high percentage of people who suffer from eating disorders have a history of sexual abuse, and a high percentage of individuals who have a history of sexual abuse engage in self-injury.

DISSOCIATIVE DISORDERS

The dissociative disorders are a cluster of disorders that are characterized by an experience of detachment from the environment. One of the most well-known dissociative disorders is dissociative identity disorder, formerly known as "multiple personality disorder." Individuals with dissociative disorders have typically experienced severe trauma in early childhood, typically repeated sexual abuse. The dissociative disorders are rare, so a thorough evaluation can determine whether your child suffers from any of them. It is more common, however, for a child to experience some dissociation during a cutting episode, even though she may not suffer from a dissociative disorder. These kind of dissociative experiences can be both a trigger for and a result of cutting.

The self-injury that occurs in relation to these disorders is often a way for the individual to "bring herself back" to reality when losing touch with the present moment. Many self-injurers describe physical pain or the sight of blood as evidence that they are alive.

POST-TRAUMATIC STRESS DISORDER

Post-traumatic stress disorder (PTSD) is an anxiety disorder that occurs as a result of exposure to a very traumatic incident in which the person's life was threatened or the person was physically harmed. Typical triggers include military combat, rape, physical assault, and natural disasters. Individuals with PTSD typically experience nightmares, flashbacks of the traumatic incident, difficulty regulating mood, feeling detached from life and others, an exaggerated startle response, amnesia, sleep difficulties, emotional numbness, avoidance of situations or conversations related to the event, physical symptoms of anxiety, and a lack of interest in daily life. Self-injury that occurs as a result of PTSD is typically done in order to escape the painful memories, cope with feelings of numbness, and/or regulate emotions. Inflicting physical pain can be a powerful distraction from the often-painful flashbacks—physical pain replaces the emotional pain. And, as in the dissociative disorders, physical pain can also help the person return to "reality" if they are feeling detached from themselves or their environment. Self-injury can also be a powerful regulator of emotions for people experiencing a jumble of feelings that they can't express or understand.

BIPOLAR DISORDER

Bipolar disorder, or manic depression, is a type of mood disorder that involves vacillating between manic or hypomanic episodes and depressive episodes. A manic episode is characterized by a distinct period in which the person displays a dramatic change in her behavior characterized by elevated, expansive, and irritable mood. The person typically displays grandiosity, decreased need for sleep, increased talking, and risky behavior, such as excessive spending and unsafe sexual practices. A hypomanic episode is similar to a manic episode but with symptoms that are less severe. With a hypomanic episode, the person's daily life is also not impaired to the same degree as is typically seen in mania. Individuals with mania manifest more severe behavioral disturbances, which lead to more significant functional impairment. For example, a person with hypomania may just overspend on impulse buys, whereas a person in a manic episode is more likely to max out every credit card. A major depressive episode is a distinct period of extreme sadness, loss of interest or pleasure in previously enjoy activities, suicidal thoughts, decreased concentration and thinking abilities, sleep and appetite disturbances, and a change in activity level.

There are two major types of bipolar disorders: bipolar I and bipolar II. Individuals with bipolar I have a history of at least one manic episode and may or may not have experienced a major depressive episode. Individuals with bipolar II, on the other hand, have had at least one major depressive disorder and at least one hypomanic episode.

As in major depression, people with bipolar disorder experience mood changes, but unlike depressed patients they may also seem manic at times. In fact, the word "manic" is often used to describe an ordinary person who is so busy that he or she never seems to stop and rest. A manic episode in bipolar disorder, however, is much more than just being productive and energized. Individuals in a manic episode are clearly suffering from a serious condition. They may seem out of touch with reality, their speech may be quite rapid, and they may skip from one topic to another. They may tell you that they are the best in the world at what they do. They may be argumentative, demanding, and hostile. They typically engage in high-risk behaviors and do not consider the consequences. They have a significantly decreased need for sleep; they may spend an hour on the treadmill after sleeping for just two hours and then work or study for the entire day without experiencing any fatigue. If you notice any of these signs in your child, especially if they seem to appear suddenly, then it is important to seek immediate psychiatric help.

Individuals in a manic episode can place themselves at risk very quickly. Suicide attempts are quite common in individuals with bipolar disorder. If you sense that your child is endangering herself or others as a result of a manic episode, especially if she is also expressing suicidal thoughts, then taking her to the hospital emergency room may be the best course of action. Otherwise, consider making an immediate appointment with a psychiatrist or psychopharmacologist for medication. Once your child has begun taking medication, seek psychological treatment to address the illness as well as the self-injury.

Self-injury that occurs in the context of bipolar disorder is likely an attempt at mood regulation. However, the type of self-injury may vary based on whether the individual is manic or depressed at the time. Self-injury that occurs in the context of mania tends to be more dangerous and life threatening than injury that occurs during a depressive episode. Individuals with bipolar disorder have significantly higher rates of suicide attempts and completed suicides, so their self-injurious behaviors may be more severe or may tend to coincide with suicidal behaviors as well. It is extremely important to seek immediate medical attention if you suspect that your child may have a mood disorder, as her self-injury could be a sign of growing risk to her health and life.

MAJOR DEPRESSION

Major depression, or clinical depression, is characterized by a complex constellation of symptoms that include extreme sadness, irritability, changes in sleep and appetite, suicidal thoughts or attempts, impaired concentration, impaired problem-solving skills and memory, poor body image, feelings of worthlessness and guilt, fatigue, decreased interest in sexual activity, lack of interest in previously pleasurable activities, general apathy, and physical agitation or slowness. Individuals with major depression experience distinct episodes in which they experience five or more of the mentioned symptoms for at least a two-week period. The duration and frequency of episodes can vary from one individual to another. Some individuals might experience depressive episodes that last for three months and then remain in recovery for years before experiencing a second episode, while others experience many episodes in any given year.

Sadness and depression are a normal part of the human experience. It would be rare to encounter someone who has not had a period of depressed mood during or following a loss or traumatic change in his or her life. Teenagers especially may experience frequent changes in mood or feelings of depression. The distinction between sadness and major depression is based on the intensity and duration of the depressed mood. The mood must be persistent (lasting at least two weeks), occur for a majority of your child's day, and impact her daily functioning in order for it to be classified as major depression. Does she have difficulty getting out of bed in the morning? Has she begun to isolate herself from her friends? Has she given up all of the activities she previously enjoyed? Does she seem particularly angry or irritable? Does she become easily upset by the slightest things? Has her sleep and appetite changed for no apparent reason? These are all indicators that your child may be suffering from major depression rather than just feeling blue.

Major depression affects up to 18 million adults in the United States in any given year and greatly impacts the U.S. economy. New estimates suggest that depression costs the U.S. approximately $83 billion in 2000. Of that total, $26.1 billion is in direct medical costs, $5.4 billion for suicide related mortality, and $51.5 billion in workplace costs (Greenberg et al. 2003). Depression can occur in any stage of life and can be a result of environmental stressors, genetics, or medical illnesses such as thyroid and hormonal dysfunctions.

Besides being its own separate diagnostic entity, depression is a common symptom associated with a variety of mental illnesses, including all of the ones mentioned above. Symptoms of depression often complicate and interfere with the effectiveness of mental health treatment of other disorders. An individual who is depressed may be tired or hopeless and therefore may be reluctant to engage in treatment or comply with a prescribed daily medical regime. Although new medications and treatment options for depression are available, this illness continues to challenge mental health professionals.

Because depression is such a complex condition, self-injurious behavior may be a result of any of a variety of factors. Each individual with depression presents in a slightly different way, just as no two humans are alike. Therefore, self-injury in one person may be due to a sense of hopelessness about the future, while in another individual it may function as self-punishment for past errors or as a release from constant emotional pain.

Cognitive Style: Perfectionistic Thinking

Individuals who self-injure, regardless of the specific diagnostic category they fit into, exhibit certain cognitive styles of thinking. Everyone has a particular thinking style. We all have certain ways in which we think, evaluate, and perceive ourselves and the world around us. Certain styles of thinking are more flexible and adaptive and help us cope and adjust to the world around us. People who view things in a balanced and rational fashion tend to be more emotionally healthy and able to cope with adversity as well as the daily challenges of life. People with emotional disturbances tend to think less flexibly, which predisposes them to experience more unpredictable and extreme negative emotions.

One style of particularly inflexible thinking is perfectionism. While we all want to do our best, and we encourage our children to do the same, there is a vast difference between healthy achievement orientation and pathological perfectionism. Some individuals are so focused on doing things perfectly, looking perfect, or on achieving perfect performance that their relentless pursuit of their superhuman goals really begins to interfere with normal functioning. Many of the cutters we work with share this type of maladaptive perfectionism in one or more areas of their lives. They have internalized the belief that unless they act, look, or perform perfectly they are not doing their best and are therefore unlovable and unworthy of praise or attention.

Sadly, instead of motivating individuals to achieve more, pathological or maladaptive perfectionism leads to crushing disappointments when anything less than perfection is obtained, the inability to enjoy any achievement unless it is perfect, and self-punishment. The problem is that the likelihood of always achieving success and being the best diminishes the more we try to achieve. So, pathological perfectionists wind up passing on a lot of opportunities, or avoiding a lot of potential growth experiences, in order to avoid failing (which becomes tantamount to achieving anything less than perfection).

Maladaptive perfectionism is a component of several types of psychopathologies, including, but not limited to, eating disorders, obsessive-compulsive disorder, body dysmorphic disorder, depression, and even suicidality. What really distinguishes maladaptive from adaptive perfectionism is the ability to tolerate failure well, and to learn from it in a constructive way. Maladaptive perfectionists tend to melt down when they fail, feeling as if they have lost their only shot at redemption and that they can't go on in the face of failure.

The behavioral consequences of maladaptive perfectionism include extreme slowness in approaching or completing tasks, frequent failure to complete tasks, procrastination, avoidance of trying new things or any activity where the outcome of 100 percent success cannot be guaranteed, and, eventually, self-punishment if goals are not met with 100 percent success. When pathological perfectionists fail to achieve perfection (such as earning a 94 instead of a 100 on a test), they consider it a failure. When one's standards are that high, a slight misstep leaves one with miles to fall. Those falls are often punished with relentless psychological self-flagellation, which may eventually become physical. When it does, it can manifest as self-injury.

BIOLOGICAL BASES OF SELF-INJURY

Self-injury seems to be an emotionally triggered behavior, so why would anyone be interested in its biological bases? Well, think about it: we all experience some intense negative emotions in our lifetimes, so why don't we all cut in response to them? Part of the answer lies in our brain chemicals and hormones.

Several theories explain the biological bases of self-injury. We will look at the most commonly accepted ones to see how certain brain chemicals and hormones can either increase or inhibit self-injury. You may find this information valuable in helping you understand how the medications prescribed by your child's psychiatrist work to treat self-injury.

The Serotonin Link ·

Serotonin, or 5-HT, is a neurochemical that seems to serve many different regulatory functions in the human brain and body. Serotonin regulates our appetite, sleep, and sex drive, but, more important, it seems to play a major regulatory role in our mood: if levels of serotonin are too low, or if there are too few receptor sites to keep sufficient amounts traveling at an efficient speed, we can become depressed. It also regulates our anxiety levels (again, if there is too little present, or if it travels inefficiently, we are more prone to anxiety and obsessive thinking). Some researchers have also found that lower levels of serotonin may be linked to irritability and anger as well as an increased impulsivity and aggression, particularly self-aggression (Herpertz, Sass, and Favazza 1997). In several studies of individuals with histories of chronic suicidality and self-injury, researchers found that lower levels of serotonin correlated with increased impulsivity and aggression (specifically aggression with the self as the target) (McKay, Kulchycky, and Danyko 2000; New et al. 1997; Oquendo and Mann 2000).

When we take this fact into consideration, it makes sense that individuals who self-injure report higher levels of depression and anxiety, due to lower levels of serotonin, which may be manifesting themselves in the form of anger, irritability, and impulsivity in addition to self-injurious behavior. In addition, research also suggests that self-injury is related to obsessive-compulsive symptoms, with serotonin deficiencies cited as the common link (McKay, Kulchycky, and Danyko 2000), which is why self-injury often takes on a ritualistic pattern and can become a compulsive act if repeated. A serotonergic imbalance may account for your adolescent's mood dysregulation, and why she might also be reporting (or you might be observing) higher levels of depression and/or anxiety.

Often, psychiatrists will prescribe medications called SSRIs (selective serotonin reuptake inhibitors), examples of which are Prozac, Zoloft, Lexapro, Luvox, and Celexa, to increase the levels of available serotonin in the brain. (Paxil is also an SSRI, but it is currently contra-indicated for use in children or adolescents.) These medications are often referred to as antidepressants, but they can address a variety of symptoms related to mood, anxiety, obsessionality, and compulsivity, as well as agitation and impulsivity. These medications may affect sleep, appetite, and sexual drive, since these are also serotonin-related functions.

The Endogenous Opiate Hypothesis

Endogenous opiates, or endorphins, are the brain's pleasure chemicals, the ones that produce feelings of well-being, are associated with "runner's high," and are produced when we are injured to keep us from feeling too much pain. Some research indicates that individuals who engage in self-injury have lower levels of these pleasure chemicals, and that their acts of self-injury actually serve to restore these levels to normal (Oquendo and Mann 2000; Russ 1992; Winchel and Stanley 1991). In fact, in self-injurers, it may actually take an act of self-injury to release endorphins that would help to end an aversive mood state.

This is where the affect regulation model of self-injury comes in. Individuals who self-injure may be more predisposed toward negative mood because of lower levels of circulating endorphins. The only way that they can end a negative mood is to injure themselves, leading to an endorphin rush, which immediately leads to feelings of relief, increased relaxation, and improved mood.

The above-described cycle is likely the reason that self-injury is addictive in nature. The pleasant feeling, or opiate response, that occurs as a result of self-injury wears off and the individual feels the need to repeat the act. Eventually, according to the addiction hypothesis, chronic overstimulation of this system leads to increased "tolerance" of the opiate response and an increased need to self-injure. As Armando Favazza (1998) states, somewhere between the twentieth and thirtieth cut self-injury may take on an addictive quality.

In addition, the pain hypothesis suggests that problems in the biological regulation of pleasure chemicals (our bodies' own opiates, or endorphins) may lead to an increased pain threshold (which is why self-injurers need to cut more frequently and intensely over time, and why some cutters report less pain than others during cutting). In turn, the imbalance of endorphins may lead to the increased likelihood of experiencing numbness and dissociation (because these brain chemicals are being released inappropriately or in an untimely fashion), which can only be broken by self-injury. These would be described as the individuals who "cut to feel."

A few psychiatrists will prescribe medications that increase endogenous opiate levels in the brain for self-injurers. However, much less research on this theory has been done than on the relationship between serotonin and self-injury, so many practitioners are more comfortable prescribing SSRIs.

Cortisol and Norepinephrine: Hyperactivity of the Body's Stress Response in Self-Injurers

A small number of researchers (New et al. 1997; Sachsse, Von Der Heyde, and Huether 2002) have also implicated cortisol, a chemical released by our adrenal glands when we are under stress, as a biological correlate to self-injury. It is suggested that some individuals who self-injure may do so in response to increasing levels of cortisol.

Essentially, researchers theorize that people who self-injure may have lower levels of cortisol, which may make them more reactive to subtle increases in this stress chemical. This may explain why those who self-injure seem more vulnerable to what we would consider smaller environmental or emotional triggers. In any case, increases in cortisol levels may be linked to increased negative emotionality and may lead to self-injury. In addition, cortisol levels may decrease in response to self-injury (Sachsse, Von Der Heyde, and Huether 2002), leading to a reduction in anxiety or tension.

Norepinephrine (or noradrenaline) is another of our body's stress chemicals that is manufactured and secreted by the adrenal glands. Norepinephrine is one of the chemicals released during the "fight-or-flight" response, the body's reaction to perceived threat. Lower levels of norepinephrine have been associated with increased inhibition and lower levels of aggression, while increased levels are associated with impulsivity and aggressive behavior. Increased norephinephrine release has been noted among those who self-injure and is associated with the impulsivity and more intense emotional reactivity of self-injurious individuals.

As we've seen, cortisol and norepinephrine, both produced by the endocrine glands (adrenals), are released when the body is under stress. In individuals who self-injure, there may be what Ulrich Sachsse and colleagues (2002) refer to as "hyperactivity of the central stress-sensitive neuroendocrine systems." In plain English, this means that those who self-injure may not just be more emotionally reactive but also more biologically reactive as well. Therefore, they may be more vulnerable to negative emotional states and stressful environmental events than the average individual. In addition, they may react more intensely to these triggers and may tend to be more impulsive and aggressive, self-injuring to regulate their aversive emotional states.

Self-injury can be the result of a variety of psychological and or biological disturbances. Understanding the particular contributing factors for your child's self-injury can increase the odds that she will receive proper treatment. For example, if your child is bipolar but is not receiving the right types of medication, then the best therapy in the world could fail to help her. For this reason, it is highly important that you seek the help of a trained mental health professional if you have any concerns at all about your child's well-being.

3

Environmental Factors in Self-Injury

Self-injury can have roots in forces external to an individual as well as in the internal factors discussed in the previous chapter. The emotional climate in your home, the television and movies that your child watches, even his friends and the very culture he lives in can influence his responses to emotional distress and whether or not he will react by self-injuring. In this chapter, we will examine the impact of culture and social influences in the development of self-injury in your child.

ANTHROPOLOGICAL AND HISTORICAL ASPECTS OF SELF-INJURY

Adolescence is, historically, a time of change. As maturation progresses, physical changes become prominent, as do changes in attitude, behavior, and thinking. Extant primitive cultures are our most valuable window into our ancient history, and therein we can find clues about our current conceptualizations about many aspects of our everyday lives. Adolescence, in many primitive cultures and in our own modern world, is often viewed as a rite of passage, and, although many of the ceremonies that formerly marked this momentous time in human development have died out, we can look to primitive rituals to find clues that explain some confusing behaviors in modern society.

One of the significant events in a pubescent female's development is menstruation. Culturally, menstruation has been viewed as both a mysterious time, when a girl develops the awesome power of reproduction, and as a negative time, when she loses her innocence and develops the potential to become a depraved person subject to her most base (sexual) desires. In either case, the menstrual flow signifies a substance endowed with supernatural powers. Actions may be taken to sanctify the female and her menstrual blood (as in primitive African cultures, where the menstruating female and her blood are looked at as magical and potent and are treated with veneration). Alternatively, the female and the genitalia from which the menstrual blood emerges may be viewed as base and dangerous (as in certain cultures that mark menstruation with a slap in the face, the imposition of more restrictive and less revealing garments, or even female circumcision, which involves the removal of the clitoris and/or labia minora).

Since the time of the first recognition that males were also necessary in the reproductive process, which occurred in the Neolithic era, scarification ceremonies have emerged as a pubertal ritual. Essentially, when males recognized that they too possessed some power to create the life force, rites of passage for males, involving bloodletting of the genitalia (achieved by cutting the penis) to simulate the female menstruation, were conducted. What does this have to do with adolescent self-injury? Well, everything.

Think about it: adolescence has been historically associated with bloodletting, the ability to tolerate increased pain (whether from menstrual cramps or cutting of the male genitalia), and the increased maturity and respect that result from enduring these events. In fact, adolescents have learned that the ability to control one's body and the pain that it undergoes are very much adult capacities. Ritual scarification is only one example of such behavior.

As we've seen in the discussion above, sometimes culturally sanctioned behaviors and rituals can look like self-injury, though they're actually just popular cultural trends that give individuals an outlet to express their personalities or viewpoints. Parents in every generation watch their children adopt the current fashion trends and wonder to themselves, "How could this possibly be considered attractive?" The parents of the current generation are no different. Since the punk rock movement began in the late 1970s, several generations of parents have watched in horror as body piercings have increased in popularity. Every part of the body, including eyebrows, noses, belly buttons, and even nipples and genitalia, has fallen prey to implements from safety pins to small metal barbells. Some teenagers even seem to be addicted to this practice and seek out more and more piercings, never seeming to be satisfied. Many of the parents that we come in contact with in the course of treating teens ask us if body piercing and tattooing should be a cause for concern.

In addition, recent media attention has focused on a behavior that at first glance appears to be blatantly self-injurious. The behavior in question is the "choking game," also referred to as the "passing-out game." Essentially, adolescents have been "playing" at cutting off the oxygen supply to their brains in order to achieve a narcotic-like high. During the summer of 2005, the choking game resulted in the accidental deaths of several youths. But can this actually be classified as a self-injurious behavior?

The type of self-injury we are discussing herein is not a "culturally sanctioned" behavior. So, according to our definition, current fashion trends that are widely accepted, such as body piercing or tattooing, are not considered examples of self-injurious behavior. And, while we consider intentional asphyxia to be an extremely dangerous cultural trend, we do not consider it to be self-injury, because it is not intended to cause harm and is done in order to feel high, or good. True self-injury, like any other behavior associated with psychological disturbance, is generally the result of extreme negative emotions and causes significant impairment in that individual's daily functioning.

Adults in cultures throughout the world, even today, engage in behaviors that may seem to cause deliberate harm to the body; many of these cultural rituals have been practiced for millennia. However, because they are widely accepted rituals within that social group, the behavior is not considered abnormal. For example, because a long neck is considered highly attractive within the Ndebele and Padaung cultures in South Africa and Burma, respectively, the women in these groups wear wire coils around their neck in an attempt to weigh down their collarbones and give the appearance of an elongated neck (Koda 2001). Similarly, some women in the Chinese culture bind their feet in order to make them smaller, a practice thought to have originated around the tenth century. Although these body-altering techniques have been used to achieve an esthetically pleasing body, tribes and cultures also engage in rituals that deliberately harm the body for the purpose of healing and spirituality. These rites tend to be rich in symbolism and meaning within the cultural group. Self-injury, on the other hand, holds meaning to the individual engaging in the behavior but not to the entire culture.

However, this is not always the case. In 1789 the crew of the British ship *Pandora* documented the ritual self-injury of Tahitian islanders, as a rite of mourning, after the seizure and departure of the *Bounty* mutineers, with whom the islanders had intermarried and started families. The distraught Tahitians reportedly surrounded the *Pandora* in canoes, stripped their clothing, and bashed their heads with broken shells in a culturally sanctioned display of grief. It was believed by the islanders that such a display would influence the crew of the *Pandora* to release their beloved mutineers (Alexander 2003). Other explorers and naval visitors to the Tahitian Islands during the eighteenth century also witnessed and reported on similar events. Apparently, this behavior was a culturally sanctioned, ritualistic form of self-injury, performed not for the express purpose of inflicting pain but as part of a mourning display. The behavior, then, was meaningful as a collective cultural act, not as an individual act.

The self-injury practice known as corporal mortification performed by many canonized Catholic saints was viewed as a sign of their repentance, a means of relieving guilt and ridding themselves of their sins through self-punishment in prostration to their omnipotent God. It was also considered a means of demonstrating love for God through toleration of extreme self-inflicted pain. Throughout history these individuals have been revered and, in fact, sanctified. However, they self-injured for many of the same reasons that some adolescents do today. Through self-injury they were able to achieve relief from mental torture, to repent for sins (real or imagined), to build strength and character, and to feel in control, at least of their own spiritual fate.

Historically and culturally, self-injury is considered to be a problematic behavior when it does not have meaning within an entire cultural group, when it is the result of psychological disturbance, and when it interferes with the person's daily functioning. Self-injury in adolescents is a socially unacceptable behavior, driven by psychological turmoil or upset, that becomes a maladaptive method for coping with painful emotions, eventually leading to severe problems in daily functioning and potentially to grave injury or even death.

PEER INFLUENCES ON SELF-INJURY

One basic rule of thumb that we adhere to in our clinical work is that nobody can *make* a person cut. We really believe in empowering the adolescents we work with by having them own the responsibility for their self-injury. This is not to say that we blame them, or that we discount the reality that certain individuals or settings can be definite triggers for self-injury. We are simply saying that the actual act of cutting is a behavioral choice that is within each person's power (even though sometimes it doesn't seem like it) to choose or reject.

Having said that, we also recognize that many of the adolescents we work with feel as if they are "floundering in a sea of pain" (as one very articulate fifteen-year-old girl stated). Because they feel too embarrassed or afraid to confide in parents or other family members about their behavior, they may rely on their peers as their sole source of support. However, their peers may be extremely ill-equipped to deal with their friends' pain or self-injurious behavior. In fact, many adolescents who self-injure have problematic peer relationships, which may lead them to feel that they are at the mercy of friends who are sharing similar emotional experiences, or with whom they do not share stable relationships. Thus, teens who are self-injuring and whose primary support group is composed of peers who may be doing the same are more likely to continue this behavior and are less likely to get the help that they need.

Often, we find that adolescents who self-injure tend to cluster together, probably because they can understand and match each other's levels of emotional intensity, can relate to one another's pain, and can discuss their self-injury openly, without the fear of being misunderstood or rejected as they might be with other peers. Cutters tend to find solace in bonding with other cutters, or those who are engaging in similarly destructive behaviors. It seems that they bond with each other not through specific, injurious behaviors but through the shared understanding of the intense, painful, negative emotions or experiences that have triggered their self-injury in the first place.

There is a phenomenon that we refer to as "copycat cutting," which is basically the spread of imitative cutting within peer groups and may be a source of worry for parents. However, seeing someone else's injuries, watching him self-injure, or hearing about his self-injury episodes is *not enough*, in and of itself, to make your child cut. We believe that if one is not biologically predisposed to self-injury (see chapter 2) then one might engage in brief experimentation or imitation of a peer's cutting, but the behavior will not "stick" the way it would in an individual whose brain is already hardwired for self-injury. Generally, the adolescents we work with—the adolescents who have engaged in self-injury in a way that is much more than just experimentation—report that prior to their first episode of cutting they had observed or heard about self-injury from a close relative or peer. Though they might have initially been shocked by the revelation, they report that it somehow resonated with them, and that they could not forget about their exposure to it and thought about it a lot before actually trying it. The other difference between predisposed cutters and those who simply dabble in it is their physiological and emotional reaction to it in the early stages of self-injury. Those who seem to have a basic hardwired predilection for such behaviors report some blunted pain and marked relief from emotional tension during the first episode of cutting, and even some elation. Those for whom cutting is a one-shot deal indicate more pain and discomfort (both psychological and biological) and less relief as a result of their attempts at cutting. However, it is possible for an individual who is not biologically predisposed to cutting to become a true cutter, due to sheer repetition and social reinforcement. Below is an example of a fifteen-year-old who copied her cousin's behavior and began to cut. Though she was, in fact, probably biologically predisposed to become a cutter (with a family history of self-injury and anxiety), having a behavioral model likely served as a trigger for her cutting at that point in time.

▪ Naomi's Story

When Naomi was fifteen, she attended a holiday dinner with her parents and extended family. Due to the extremely boring "adult" conversation going on at the dinner table, she and her fourteen- and sixteen-year-old female cousins snuck off to hang out on the roof of the house, try her older cousin's cigarettes, and talk about teen-relevant topics.

During a conversation about school and boyfriends, Naomi's older cousin revealed that she had just broken up with her boyfriend of nine months. She said that she'd been really upset and had contemplated suicide. When Naomi asked what she had done to cope, her cousin stated that she had been getting drunk and had been cutting. Naomi initially thought she meant that she had been cutting classes, but then her cousin showed Naomi her upper arms, which were scarred with many faint, symmetrical scars and some fresh cuts. Then she pulled a tiny pair of scissors from her purse and demonstrated for the others to see. Naomi said she was initially very disturbed by this behavior, but she also stated that she just couldn't forget about it. She never told her parents about any of it, because she thought that she would get in trouble for being on the roof and smoking.

She thought about that conversation with her cousin every day for weeks, and she couldn't get the image of her cousin cutting out of her mind. She began to trace lines on her ankles, imagining that she was cutting while she did it, but never intending to actually cut.

That summer, Naomi began feeling depressed. She had done poorly in school for the first time ever and had to attend a summer class. She had been fighting with her mother and father about her attitude and always seemed to be at odds with her friends, who kept accusing her of "turning into a weirdo." As Naomi became increasingly alienated from her family and friends, she thought more and more about cutting. One night in late summer, after being bashed by her friends online, Naomi felt so distraught that she actually thought of killing herself—her "turning point." Almost five years later, Naomi still vividly recalls going into her bathroom, running the water to cover any sounds that she might make, and cutting her ankles about twenty times each in tiny, perfect parallel lines until she felt nothing at all. She describes feeling "total relief" mixed with "total numbness."

For the next five months, unbeknownst to her family, Naomi cut herself every day, moving from her ankles to her hips when she ran out of room. She stopped associating with all of her old friends and began hanging out with a girl she had previously regarded as too weird to be friends with. This girl, who was also a cutter, ultimately persuaded Naomi to tell her mother about her self-injury.

Naomi entered treatment almost a year after she had seen her cousin cut. She eventually stopped cutting regularly, after about five months of therapy, but experienced strong, "irresistible" self-injurious thoughts every few months over the next two years. Naomi is now in college and has not cut in over two years, but she says she still remembers the experience clearly. Occasionally, when she is experiencing a lot of stress, she craves cutting, but she is now able to resist the urge.

FAMILY INFLUENCES ON SELF-INJURY

Just as increased rates of self-injury in adolescents may be associated with certain types of peer groups (for example, countercultures in which cutting is an acceptable form of self-expression, such as Goths, or those groups that are made up of self-injurers), we also see increased rates of self-injury occurring in certain family environments. Of course, we do not blame families for their adolescents' self-injury, nor do we believe that there is some classic type of family environment that promotes cutting. However, we do find that certain types of family situations or attitudes go along with increased numbers of children and teens who self-injure.

Below we discuss some family factors that can play a role when an adolescent is self-injuring.

Divorce and Dysfunction

Though we know that more than half of all American marriages currently result in divorce, it doesn't seem that children or teens are getting used to the concept of family dissolution. Many children and teens cite divorce as a significant turning point in their lives, since divorce generally brings many changes that occur without children's input or control. In addition, many children and adolescents whose parents divorce experience what they may perceive as an immediate loss of emotional support when one parent moves away. The resultant fighting, family tension, and separation that come with a divorce can be extremely difficult on the minors involved. This emotional strain can be compounded by the major practical and logistical changes that may also occur, such as moving out of the family home or to a different area, and issues related to moving (starting a new school, losing old friends, and so on).

For many children and even teenagers with a latent but lurking predisposition to develop mood issues, anxiety problems, obsessive-compulsive symptoms, or impulse-control problems, the stress of a particularly tumultuous family situation, particularly one culminating in a divorce, may be the straw that breaks the camel's back—the direct trigger for emotional problems and self-injury.

So, does divorce make children cut? No. However, it can make them feel out of control, insecure, and lacking in support, and it may cause them to blame themselves. Therefore, if divorce really is the best option, we advise parents to think of their children's needs at least as much as their own and to seek professional intervention at every step in order to approach the change in the least damaging way possible. When children's pain is ignored, they will find ways (usually shocking and unhealthy ones) to *show* people how much pain they're in. Cutting is just one of the methods that children and adolescents can use to cry out for help, and it is certainly one of the most dangerous.

In particularly negative family situations, where physical, sexual, or emotional abuse is occurring, where a parent is abusing substances, or where intense anger or discord is present, divorce may actually be the healthiest option. In fact, in such situations, it could be more damaging for the children or adolescents involved to be exposed to the ongoing toxicity of that environment. If the family environment is an extremely dysfunctional one, then maintaining the status quo (staying together for the children, for financial reasons, or for the purpose of avoiding social stigma) can create just as much, if not more, emotional havoc in the children's lives. Children and teens who are exposed to repeated conflict and trauma, are ignored and invalidated, or experience little perceived control over their daily lives are likely to seek to control the things that they can, such as their bodies. In this case, cutting is just one way of getting back a feeling of control, and it is also a way to escape from the pain and to "numb out." So, just as we do with divorcing parents, we also ask these parents to think of their children and their emotional needs and to ask themselves if staying together is worth risking their children's physical and emotional safety.

Perfectionism

What does an adolescent's family environment have to do with perfectionism? Well, some perfectionists are born, and some are made. It is well known that certain people have a significant genetic predisposition to develop specific disorders such as obsessive-compulsive disorder, anorexia, and depression, so it makes sense that perfectionism, an element of these disorders, could run in families. However, when children are continuously exposed to maladaptive levels of parental or familial perfectionism that they observe being reinforced and rewarded, they may actually learn to set for themselves the same kinds of rigid, unattainable goals. They learn that this is the "right" way to behave. Then, when they cannot achieve those goals, they experience a feeling of total failure. When these children or adolescents are under the impression that they have completely failed at some important aspect of life, they tend to become despondent and are more likely to engage in self-injury.

In these cases, we suggest a two-pronged approach. First, we examine the child's maladaptive perfectionistic thinking and related behaviors. We target the beliefs that maintain these behaviors, and we ask the child to test out the beliefs to find out if they are really logical and true (for example, "I have to study for twelve hours for every test, because if I don't, I won't get an A, and then my parents will hate me"). First, using the example above, we would have the child study for substantially less than twelve hours; then we'd see what kind of grade he achieved. Next, we'd have that child pick a class that he was doing very well in and have him not study for a test or try not to get a perfect score in order to see if his parents, in fact, hated him (which is generally not the case). At the same time, we'd ask the parents to work with one of our other therapists to do the very same experiment in their own lives, so that they could support their child in the process of therapy and begin modeling healthier thinking and behaviors at home.

In another type of situation that we frequently observe, parents or other family members attempt to *teach* their own pathological perfectionism to their children, with no recognition of their own faulty reasoning and maladaptive coping styles. When this occurs, the fallout is equally bad and tends to be a source of significant parent-child conflict. In such cases, we have encountered children and adolescents who possess pretty reasonable expectations about their own performance or appearance but are continually told by their disappointed parents that they "expect better" (which, when examined, generally translates to "nothing less than the best"). We have had parents sit in our offices berating their children for bringing home improved but imperfect report cards—who argue with us when we explain that their child is doing better and that improvement (not perfection) is the goal. These parents have told us that this is "loser thinking" and will never lead to any kind of substantial achievement in life. To this we respond, "Way to motivate your child. Not!" If a child's efforts at improvement are met with further criticism or simply a lack of recognition, then that child will likely stop trying. When a child gets the message that he is unable to please his parents, or that he constantly disappoints them, he tends to view himself as a failure. This negative self-concept makes unhealthy decisions, like taking safety risks and engaging in dangerous behaviors like cutting, that much easier. Think of it this way: if you are, at the tender age of thirteen, already a failure and a loser in your parents' eyes, then what do you really have to lose by cutting or doing anything else maladaptive or dangerous?

When perfectionistic parents are resistant to working on changing their own beliefs and actions because they see nothing wrong with them, it is certainly a more difficult situation. It's absolutely essential for us to help such parents begin to see how their beliefs and attitudes (and the behavioral and verbal manifestations of them) are harming their children. Our approach to this is to clearly state the following: "Your child is suffering and you are contributing to his suffering. He will never look, behave, or perform perfectly. Either you can accept that and begin praising the good things that he does, in hope of improving his self-esteem and eventually his achievement level, or you can keep doing exactly what you are doing, which will just lead him to feel much worse about himself, alienate him from you, and contribute to further self-injury. The power to change is in your hands."

SEXUAL ABUSE

In the introduction to this book, we stated that children and adolescents who are sexually abused are significantly more likely to engage in self-injury. Researchers cite dissociation as the mechanism that connects these two issues (McKay, Kulchycky, and Danyko 2000; Rodriguez-Srednicki 2001). Essentially, when sexual abuse occurs, particularly in children and adolescents (but also in adult victims of rape and sexual brutality), dissociation or disconnection sets in as a protective mechanism. If full awareness, or connectedness between one's physical, emotional, and conscious experience, means that one would feel the full impact of the pain on all levels during abuse, then dissociation, or the disconnectedness between one's body, emotions, and conscious experience, would numb the victim to some of that pain. Similar phenomena are noted when individuals experience medically grave injuries, such as gunshot wounds or amputations. Victims of such traumas sometimes report initially feeling the impact or injury but then experiencing a surreal state, marked anesthesia, and the feeling that they were watching the scene from a third-person perspective. This is, in essence, the very nature of dissociation. It's the brain's way of protecting us from events and experiences that it identifies as too painful or traumatic for us to be fully present for.

The problem with dissociation is that it's wonderful for short-term protection from trauma but isn't beneficial over the long term. If a person dissociates every time he is about to recall traumatic incidents and memories (as in post-traumatic stress disorder), the person begins to feel numb and disconnected. This is what happens in repeated sexual abuse in childhood. Numbness and dissociation, as long-term ways of being, are incredibly uncomfortable to most individuals. This is why individuals with histories of trauma, particularly childhood sexual abuse, are thought to have much higher rates of self-injury than those without such backgrounds. Think about it: the common expression "Pinch me—I must be dreaming" comes from our basic instinct to interrupt states of diminished or altered consciousness by the infliction of pain. We instinctively know that pain is the one stimulus that is strong enough to break almost any other state we could be in. Therefore, it seems biologically logical for individuals who experience frequent dissociation to try to snap out of it by engaging in self-injury.

Consider that childhood sexual abuse inappropriately focuses an individual's attention on his or her body in a sexual way, long before the brain and body are adequately equipped for it. Therefore, it makes sense that the brain would have to develop some type of strategy to help get the individual out of the situation, in mind if not body. Hence, dissociation becomes a coping strategy for victims of childhood sexual abuse. As a result, the brain that has become accustomed to escaping through dissociation during stressful experiences may do this more often than benefits the child. The child would then self-injure to stop the dissociative experience. Furthermore, if the only thing that a child can actually control is his or her body, and that very basic right is taken away by an abuser, it is logical that the child will try to regain control by inflicting injury on that body, first to make it feel something, and second to begin to own it again, however maladaptive that may be. So, in essence, self-injury in those with histories of sexual abuse seems to make sense both biologically and emotionally. The problem is that it continues to bring pain and harm to the already injured individual, simply perpetuating the cycle of abuse.

Let's look at the experience of Monica, who resorted to self-injurious behavior because of a history of sexual abuse.

■ Monica's Story

Monica is a thirty-three-year-old woman with an eighteen-year history of self-injury. When she was four, her mother left her with relatives to find work after her divorce. Subsequently, she was raised by her mother's extended family. Between the ages of four and thirteen, she was repeatedly raped and molested by two male relatives. She was also physically and emotionally brutalized by several other family members. When she was thirteen, she left to take up residence with her mother.

Fearing her mother's rejection, Monica never reported her sexual abuse. At the age of fifteen, she began to cut her arms, breasts, and thighs. She was able to hide her injuries using strategically placed clothing and jewelry and was never found out. Monica worked very hard in school and eventually paid for her own college education and advanced degree. However, Monica continued to self-injure all the while.

When she was thirty, Monica attempted suicide by overdosing on a potentially lethal dose of medication. We began therapy with her while she was still in the hospital. She reported that she had been having flashbacks of her abuse and had been dissociating, which was causing trouble for her at her high-powered job. She had found it impossible to establish any social relationships, particularly with men. She also reported interrupted sleep every night due to nightmares and nighttime panic episodes. She had no friends, was not eating, and was cutting; apart from her job, she was barely functioning. She stated that she had previously been diagnosed with depression, but it was clear that post-traumatic stress disorder was a more appropriate diagnosis at that point.

Now, after intensive therapy, Monica has not engaged in self-injury in almost two years, and she has been actively working on dealing with her repeated traumas. She is currently working one-on-one in cognitive behavioral therapy to overcome her post-traumatic stress disorder. She still has nightmares and feels very nervous when she is alone, particularly at night, but she no longer wants to hurt or kill herself. She counts this as one of her greatest accomplishments.

MEDIA INFLUENCES

You may be concerned that media representations and discussions of self-injury have encouraged your child to self-injure. And yes, it's pretty easy to blame the media (TV, movies, radio, magazines, and video games) for many of the most negative behaviors that we engage in as a culture. They're a good target. They present us with a steady stream of some of the most negative portrayals of human behavior, which are generally glorified or, at the very least, reinforced.

While we are not blaming the media for an individual's poor behavior, we do believe that the media's portrayals of self-injury play a role. If popular, highly visible, and admired icons in a culture are presented in a particular way, or seem to endorse specific behaviors, then the most susceptible members of that culture (such as at-risk adolescents with predispositions toward those particular views or behaviors) are more likely to attend to that information and imitate those unhealthy attitudes or behaviors.

Celebrities such as Angelina Jolie, Johnny Depp, Winona Ryder, and Fiona Apple have reported that they have histories of, or currently engage in, self-injury. One has only to do an online search for "cutting" to be inundated with stories of famous people who cut. What's more, the self-injury histories of such individuals are no secret; they mention their self-injury in press and television interviews that are printed in entertainment and teen periodicals. Self-injury has also been portrayed in recent movies and television shows, including *Thirteen; Girl, Interrupted; Secretary;* and even *Seventh Heaven* (which actually devoted an entire episode to self-injury). We don't view this exposure as such a bad thing, since it helps raise awareness of cutting and may allow adolescents to recognize that their own self-injury is more common than they think, perhaps giving them the confidence to seek help. However, as with the phenomenon of copycat cutting, a teen who is biologically and psychologically predisposed toward self-injury may see it presented in a favorable light and may feel less inhibited to try the behavior.

Self-injury has not been kept completely secret up until now. Such renowned authors as Sylvia Plath and Joyce Carol Oates have been writing about self-injury since the 1960s. It is even hypothesized that Sylvia Plath, who eventually committed suicide, was probably a self-injurer; her poem "The Other" offers a brief glimpse into the world of self-injury.

The fact is, however, that just reading about celebrities' perspectives on self-injury or seeing the behavior dramatized in a movie would not likely motivate someone to check out cutting if he didn't have a predisposition toward the behavior. So, while the increase in media attention to and portrayals of cutting might be correlated with general increases in these behaviors among adolescents, we can't really say that it causes cutting as much as brings it to light.

Further, while it may be tempting to make the logical leap that your child self-injures because he saw it on TV, we disagree. If this were the case, all adolescents who have had contact with popular culture would be engaging in self-injury and a myriad of far worse behaviors. We take the position that those who are predisposed to self-injure will do so, regardless of the trigger. We also think that it is better to have the subject of self-injury out in the open and getting some media attention, because the more it is recognized as a real and dangerous behavior, the better it will be understood.

Media such as music and television have been integral in the formation of certain cultural groups, such as the punkrock movement and the Goth subculture, both of which are associated with self-injurious behavior. We do not support the idea that membership in such groups leads to self-injury. However, there may be some more subtle links between certain subcultural groups and their acceptance of self-injurious behaviors. One of these groups, in particular, is the Goths (short for "Gothic," and we're not talking Bram Stoker and Mary Shelley). An apparent outgrowth of the punk rock culture of the late 1970s and early 1980s, the Gothic counterculture emerged almost simultaneously and is generally characterized by its "anti-pop-icon" appearance and ideals. Goths are easily identified by their unisex preference for all-black clothing; use of black nail polish and lipstick; and heavy, dark eye makeup. Goths, though they may seem to be drawn to all things dark, are not Satanists as a rule. The darkness of both their appearances and philosophy is more a by-product of the depression that many Goths endorse.

But Goth is more than just a counter-fashion statement for many teens. It's a cultural statement that began in music. Similar to punk rock icons like Sid Vicious of the Sex Pistols, the idols of the Goth culture are highly emotional, often intensely angry, depressed, and disillusioned (think Morrissey of the Smiths). However, often they are also intensely intelligent, emotionally expressive, and generally talented musicians. There are the Goth purists who gravitate to classic bands like Siouxsie (pronounced "Susie") and the Banshees, and then there are the more current Goths who tend to be drawn to "emo," or emotional, rock, which is intense and seems to embody all of the powerful emotional expression and general philosophy of the Gothic culture. Oh, and did we mention that many of these artists sing about, shout about, and even engage in self-injury?

Again, no more than we believe that playing a Judas Priest album backward can make an impressionable teen commit murder (the concept is just ludicrous) do we believe that wearing dark eye makeup and listening to Siouxsie or "emo" can make someone self-injure. However, we absolutely believe that an adolescent who feels depressed and misunderstood, and who is struggling to find kindred spirits, might be drawn to certain types of music or subcultural groups that might normalize, accept, and even reinforce the teen's "abnormal" feelings and behaviors.

BODY IMAGE AND SEXUALITY

Women's bodies, as shown in the media, have been shrinking over recent decades. A figure that would once have been lauded as highly attractive (such as that of Marilyn Monroe or Jayne Mansfield) would now be considered fat, or plus sized, and somehow less sexually appealing as a result. Gradually, over the last thirty years, women in magazines, in movies, and on television have been getting thinner and thinner (though they've miraculously managed to maintain very large breasts despite their ultra-low body fat, never mind the fact that breasts are composed of at least 80 percent fat). At the same time, we are told that the average person in our society has been getting bigger and bigger.

To a lesser degree, a similar phenomenon has apparently been occurring in media portrayals of men—only they have been getting more and more ripped and muscular, so that a man who would have been considered attractive and fit in the 1960s (such as Sean Connery in his Bond years) would now be considered out of shape.

As you can see, we are being presented with less attainable and realistic representations of what we should look like if we hope to be considered beautiful and attractive to members of the opposite sex. We have become a culture obsessed with appearance, and many of us spend an inordinate amount of time trying to achieve some ideal that we are unlikely to ever approach. That'll boost the old self-esteem, won't it?

Children are beginning to diet earlier and earlier, expressing body dissatisfaction at the very tender ages of nine and ten years old. Young adolescents are beginning to request personal trainers, gym memberships, and cosmetic surgery. In short, our kids are really beginning to feel the pressure to be physiologically perfect. Some of them will recognize, probably too late, that it's not what's outside that matters most. Sadly, others who are less fortunate will buy into the myth, believing that attractiveness is next to godliness, and will become obsessed with their physical appearances. The problem is that in so doing they will not feel more beautiful; they will only become more insecure and dissatisfied with their appearances, seeing only the imperfections more acutely. Some of these individuals will develop body-based obsessions such as eating disorders or body dysmorphic disorder, experiencing less body satisfaction and viewing themselves as more disfigured and distorted than the rest of the world would see them.

For these people, the universe then begins to revolve around being thin enough or muscled enough, or having the whitest teeth, straightest nose, or sleekest thighs. For some, every waking moment is spent thinking about or trying to behaviorally modify their appearances, at the cost of everything else in their lives. Does this sound a little off to you? Well, if you believed that you could achieve physical perfection if you just tried hard enough, and that you were otherwise unacceptable, unlovable, unnoticeable, and unworthy of attention, wouldn't you try to do everything you could, too?

This is the point at which many individuals begin to sink deep into self-loathing. If you thought that your continued failure to achieve physical perfection was due to your own lack of discipline or motivation, or was somehow the result of your own failure as a person, you would probably be angry at the offending object, in this case your body. The self-injuring adolescents in our practice who also have body-based disorders report that they cut out of frustration and anger at their uncooperative or imperfect forms. Essentially, their self-injury is punishment for not being perfect.

For this reason, we think it is essential to focus on treating the body-based disorder in addition to the self-injury. We also recognize that some of the appearance values that these adolescents have learned are not just the result of media influences but have actually been taught at home. In these cases, we work with the families in order to address their collective views and beliefs about attractiveness, perfection, and the value of attaining appearance goals. Sometimes, when we are treating eating disorders, we find that the family's eating, or that of certain family members, is disordered. It is important to address these issues in all environments in the child's life; otherwise the identified adolescent will not improve, because maladaptive beliefs and behaviors will continue to be reinforced at home. Not even the best therapy can fight the influence of a home environment that reinforces body-image disturbance and related behaviors.

In the previous two chapters, we discussed some of the internal and external forces that can contribute to self-injurious behavior. Up to this point, you have been presented with multiple perspectives and hypotheses as to how and why adolescents cut. Hopefully, you have a better understanding of self-injury and feel more confident in your command of the topic. Our hope is that, as you move forward, this knowledge will help you talk more comfortably to your child about cutting and to even answer some of his questions about self-injury.

4

Consequences
of Cutting

The most obvious consequences of self-injury are the physical wounds that occur as a result of cutting. However, self-injury is preceded by emotional pain and can contribute to further descent into the emotional abyss if not dealt with. In addition, self-injury may interfere with an adolescent's ability to maintain or form close interpersonal relationships during the socially critical developmental stage known as the teenage years.

This chapter will address the multiple consequences of self-injurious behavior on both the individual and her environment.

PHYSICAL CONSEQUENCES

Our bodies belong to us, so technically, we "should" be able to do anything we want to them, right? This is an argument that we hear all the time from adolescents attempting to convince us that somehow their self-injury is more justifiable than other high-risk behaviors, like drunk driving. "Yes," we say, "technically it is your body, and you are in charge of it. However, have you thought about what you're really doing to it? Would you let someone else cut you, punch you, burn you with cigarettes, or puncture your skin with pins?" Generally, the teens we work with are repulsed when we put it this way. Also, self-injurers can be so focused on the emotional result they're hoping to achieve that they're not thinking at all about the longer-term consequences, like scabs, scars, and embarrassment over having to explain their injuries.

Injury

If you think about it, cutting is, at the very least, unsafe. The most immediate consequence is physical injury, and, depending on the cutter's experience and knowledge of anatomy (or lack thereof), a cry for help could inadvertently become a life-threatening injury. Add to that the fact that most people are not exactly in the clearest frame of mind when they decide to deal with difficult emotions or life events by self-injuring, and you end up with a potentially lethal combination of poor or impaired judgment and intentional infliction of bodily harm.

We generally find that the more impulsive the act, and the more emotionally disturbed the individual is when they cut, the more severe the injury. The worst injuries we've seen have generally been inflicted when the individuals were intoxicated or under the influence of a substance, when they were in a dissociative or "numb" state, when they were extremely emotionally distressed, when the act was highly impulsive, or when they were also suicidal at the time.

Infection

We have worked with individuals who literally keep "cutting kits," which may include sterilized razor blades, scissors, pins or knives, and antibiotic ointment and peroxide, so that they have their preferred tools at their disposal when they feel the urge to cut. Many report that this helps them feel more in control of their injury and, interestingly, "safer" about their dangerous behavior. Unfortunately, there's some logic to this line of reasoning. Individuals who cut more impulsively have to depend on materials and implements in their immediate surroundings when an urge to injure hits, which gives them less control and puts them at greater risk of infection (due to lack of sterile equipment and less opportunity for proper wound care).

In addition, because so many cutters (especially teen cutters) are embarrassed by their self-injurious behavior, they may not seek the necessary medical attention that they so desperately need, instead attempting to care for their wounds on their own. Sometimes not-so-severe injuries develop into severe infections due to lack of medical attention, and, as we all know, the consequences of untreated infections can be severe.

Scarring

Many adolescents who self-injure aren't thinking too far into the future, so they really aren't considering the scars that may result from their actions, and the impact that these will have on their lives later on. Actually, we've found that in many of our patients who are trying to give up cutting, looking at their scars can trigger further episodes of self-injury. In addition to being a constant reminder of the person's loss of control and urges to engage in self-harm, those scars carry a significant social stigma. Just think of how you would react to a person, especially a teen, with scars on her wrists or arms, for example. Would you want that person to be your child's best friend, babysitter, or prom date? What if she explained to you that her cutting was a thing of the past? Would you believe her, or would you, like most people, be wary? As you can imagine, the scars that someone acquires today can affect her for years (even decades) to come.

EMOTIONAL CONSEQUENCES

Self-injury can result in physical scars, yes, but emotional scars as well. The act of injuring one's body as a means to cope with painful emotions is a concept that's pretty difficult for most people to easily accept. Stepping over that invisible line in the sand brings with it a myriad of feelings, among them weakness, lack of control, and guilt for some, but also, paradoxically, strength, power, and an illusory sense of control. Whether the emotional consequences of self-injury are negative or positive, the one thing that we've learned from the cutters we've worked with is that the feelings that immediately follow the injury are very likely to increase the likelihood of repeated injury.

Imagine cutting, and feeling so in control of your body and brain, so strong because you were able to withstand pain, and so powerful because you were able to do something that others only cringe at. You'd very likely cut again when you felt weak, out of control, and powerless.

Imagine cutting, and feeling so weak, guilty, and out of control at doing something so shameful that it's viewed with horror and contempt by most people. You just might think you deserve to punish yourself over and over again for your transgression.

The truth is that cutting serves as a pressure release valve, and that regardless of the emotional consequence, whether it be relief from pain, or a feeling of shame, it's likely to occur again because it tends to become a coping strategy. The problem with this is that, unlike helpful coping strategies, nothing's been solved and the problems that led to the cutting episode are still there. Consider self-injury as similar to getting drunk while in a state of emotional crisis. Though the intoxication itself may relieve some emotional distress for a while, it doesn't change much in one's life and may even create additional problems; immediately upon sobering up, one may have to deal with the consequences of the drunkenness (such as guilt, shame over one's behavior when drunk, and so on), as well as the original problem.

INTERPERSONAL CONSEQUENCES

Unless one exists in a social vacuum, or is artful at camouflaging one's injuries, interpersonal reactions will occur as a result of both the self-injury itself (cuts, burns, scabs, scars) and the use of a coping strategy that never really encourages coping. Whether your child likes it or not, other people will have reactions to her injury. Maybe these reactions anger her and she'd like to avoid them, or maybe she's counting on the fact that others will show concern, interest, or disgust. Either way, it's important for you and your child to recognize that her behavior will not always result in conflict resolution, attention, or whatever motivates her self-injury, and that she cannot control what others' reactions to it will be.

Attention or Recognition

Some people who self-injure display their injuries, or at least seem to make no attempt to hide them. Does this mean that they're proud of their cutting? Not necessarily. It's more likely that they're putting their pain on display, hoping someone will notice there's a problem. Your child knows that regardless of how poorly she may be doing in school, no matter how disrespectful or noncommunicative she may be at home, there are some behaviors that a parent just can't ignore. In the absence of the ability to articulate just how much she is hurting, the child may rely on visible injuries to basically scream, on her behalf, "Look at me!" These injuries can be considered cries for help.

Now imagine that you had gone to such great lengths to solicit attention and nobody noticed, or at least nobody said anything? Can you imagine how stupid you'd feel? You might then just step up the pace and escalate your injury, so there would be no possibility of any-body (especially your parents) ignoring it. If you were an adolescent hurting enough to ask for help but unwilling to do so verbally, cutting might seem like the perfect vehicle for you to convey your rage, your pain, and your self-loathing without ever having to approach anyone to discuss your feelings.

This is why it is so important for parents to address the issue of cutting at the first visible sign. Even if your child seems angry or indignant or says that the wounds are simply cat scratches, at least she knows that you know. That knowledge alone may be enough to deter future episodes of self-injury and make it possible for the child to discuss her emotional distress. You read it right: the simple act of acknowledging the first sign of injury and making your position on it clear may actually help to stop it from happening again. (For more information on starting a dialogue, see chapter 5.) The conversation might go something like this:

Parent: Hey, I see that you have some cuts on your arm. What happened?

Child: Nothing. Um, I fell into a bush on my way home from school.

Parent: Okay, but those cuts look a little too neat to be from a bush.

Child: Whatever. Are you saying I'm a liar?

Parent: I'm saying it looks like you cut yourself.

Child: God! How could you say that? I'm not mental! Do you think I'm mental?

Parent: I think that if you did that to yourself you're probably in a lot of pain. I love you and I want to know if you're hurting before you hurt yourself.

Child: Fine, but I'm not mental!

Parent: I don't think you're mental, even if you did do that to yourself. You don't have to be mental to be in pain, and some people express their pain physically, which can be very dangerous. I just want to talk about it with you. I want to know how you feel and what's going on in your life. If things seem too big for you to deal with on your own, please know that I'm here and that I can help.

Child: Whatever.

As a parent of a child who may be self-injuring, it's important to follow up, and not to assume that just because you don't see any cuts today, your child is having a good day. It's possible that she's having a lousy day and just trying to control her behavior, or maybe she's started hiding her injuries. Don't fall into the trap of assuming that no news is good news.

Repulsion

Probably for every cutter who visibly displays her injuries hoping someone will notice and volunteer some help, there is a cutter who displays injuries in order to repel others. Some self-injurers are hoping that their appearance is so shocking and scary that people will avoid them and not ask about their cuts. Basically they're screaming, "Don't look at me!" Generally, if your injuries are blatantly self-inflicted, people will assume you're doing it for attention, or to be shocking, or because you are deeply disturbed, and those people will be more likely to avoid you. If you're in enough pain, invisibility may be exactly what you seek to achieve. Sometimes, obvious self-injury brings with it a tacit "don't ask, don't tell" code. This doesn't mean that the cutter doesn't want help; it simply means that she may be in too much pain to talk about it, she may think she's hopeless, and she is banking on the fact that others will stay away so they don't have to deal with her pain or injuries.

Whether your child is self-injuring to get or repel attention, as a parent you know that you need to approach her to talk about it, no matter how shocking or scary her injuries may be (or how repulsed you are by them). The likelihood is that if you've been ignoring your teen's obvious self-injury, then you've also had to pretty much ignore your teen (and probably some other shocking or dangerous behaviors). This doesn't mean you're a bad parent. It may just mean that you're disgusted by something that we would all consider very atypical. Maybe you don't feel equipped to deal with something so totally foreign to you, or maybe you think you don't know how to help. Maybe you feel guilty, like you made your teen hurt herself, or for ignoring the self-injury for too long. If you are reading this book, be assured that though you may feel repulsed by your child's behavior, you are a concerned parent. Please don't misinterpret your discomfort for powerlessness.

Approaching your obvious cutter can be incredibly anxiety provoking for both you and your child. Please take some time to shore yourself up emotionally beforehand, and acknowledge how uncomfortable this will be for your child as well. The dialogue might go something like this (see chapters 5 and 6 for more in-depth guidelines to approaching your child about self-injury):

Parent: I would like to talk to you about your cutting. I know I've been avoiding it. It's not that I don't care, or that

I didn't notice. I just felt like I didn't know what to say, but this conversation is important.

Child: I don't want to talk about it. I'll stop, okay?

Parent: No. It's not okay that I'm your parent and you're obviously in pain and I closed my eyes. It's also not okay to let this go any farther. Even if you stop cutting right now, there's still something hurting you deeply. I want to know about it. I want to help you.

Child: I said I don't want to talk about it. You wouldn't understand and I don't want to hear you preach at me.

Parent: I heard you say you don't want to talk about it, and I respect your feelings. I can't say I'll understand, but I can promise I won't preach. I want to hear about what's bothering you. I will just listen, unless you ask me for my input. This is really important. We can't ignore it anymore.

Child: I don't feel comfortable talking to you and you won't know what to do anyway.

Parent: Fair enough, but will you come with me to talk to someone who really understands this, so I can understand it too and so I can find out how to help you the best way?

Child: No way. If you want help, you go.

Parent: I am totally prepared to do that. I'm sure I have a lot to work on too. But I can't pretend to completely understand you and I don't want to misrepresent you, so it would be a lot better if you were there to speak for yourself.

Child: Fine. I'll agree to go once, but I can't make any promises after that.

Parent: I can't either but I'm glad you're open to the idea.

Even if you've ignored your child's self-injury up to this point, this doesn't mean that you've lost your chance. If your child is alive, it's not too late to address self-injury and the problems that cause it. Even if your child self-injures blatantly in an attempt to repel others (and stop them from approaching her), you can still help.

Guilt

Have you ever gotten into a fight with someone and wished for just a moment that you would die in an unfortunate accident or be diagnosed with a deadly disease, just to make that person feel guilty for having been so mean to you? Well, sometimes people self-injure for exactly that reason. One of the major triggers of self-injury is interpersonal conflict. In essence, they punish others for hurting them by hurting themselves.

For many cutters, self-injury is a very effective way to convey messages like "You hurt me," "You treated me unfairly," and "I'm angry with you," without ever saying a word. Sometimes it's very hard to approach others to tell them how we feel, especially if we think we're going to be invalidated, or shot down, so cutting is the perfect way to send a message without increasing one's own vulnerability with that person. You really can't fight with a cut, can you?

Also, guilt itself seems to be a very effective emotional weapon and tool. It cuts deep and hard and really drives a point home. It makes everyone uncomfortable. If particular people have really upset you, then making them feel guilty is the perfect retribution and also a great way to make them see how wrong they were, right? Well? Parents use guilt on their children all the time, to extract confessions, to get chores done, to solicit help around the house. Guilt works.

Self-injury is a most effective way to elicit guilt feelings in others if it happens right after a conflict. As a parent, you know that few things could probably get to you like your child's self-injury. If you thought that you had caused the injury, you might apologize, ask for forgiveness, or at least try to see it your child's way. This is probably what your child is hoping for—instant conflict resolution through cutting. However, if this doesn't happen, the cutting is likely to escalate or occur repeatedly, especially in the absence of other interpersonal conflict resolution strategies.

WHY SHOULD PARENTS COMMUNICATE WITH CHILDREN ABOUT SELF-INJURY?

This brings us to the discussion of what happens when cutting repeatedly goes unaddressed. If you walked around with a black eye for a week and nobody asked you what happened, you might be upset or relieved, depending on how you had obtained your black eye. However, if you walked around with a black eye for three months and nobody said anything, you would probably just wonder what was so wrong with you that nobody shared an ounce of concern about your well-being. Maybe you'd give yourself another bruise just to see if anyone would notice that one.

When consistently ignored, regardless of what motivates it, self-injury is likely to escalate. When cutting is no longer enough (see chapter 2 for a discussion of self-injury's addictive nature), self-injury can lead to suicidal gestures, or it may generalize to risk-taking behaviors such as smoking, drug and alcohol use, and unprotected or promiscuous sex. Eventually, no amount of "rush" can dull the pain. Escalation in dangerous behavior is a direct consequence of self-injury being ignored. It's that simple.

Cutting doesn't generally go away, even if you do a really good job of ignoring it. It may seem to fade out of the picture for a while, but if it worked once for your child it will work again, and, untreated, it has been shown to persist in some individuals into adulthood (Rodriguez-Srednicki 2001). As a parent, you have the power to help stop a truly unhealthy behavior that could last a lifetime. You would try to get your child to stop smoking or using drugs, wouldn't you? It's just as important to view self-injury the same way.

If you continue to ignore your child's self-injury, you risk it not only enduring but also getting worse. Cutting escalates, even to the point of suicide. Maybe you could live with your child driving too fast without wearing a seatbelt, or smoking pot, but could you live with your child killing herself? It's a gamble that you're probably not willing to take. You could choose to continue to ignore your child's self-injury, but if you've read this far, you very likely want to address it.

5

How Do I Approach My Child About Cutting?

Having read chapters 1 through 4, you're now well informed about why children and adolescents cut, so you're in a pretty good position to communicate with your child about it. We also hope that you clearly understand why talking about self-injury is important, so if your child asks you, point-blank, "Why are you asking me these questions?" you'll be able to explain why the cutting conversation is so critical.

Now, you just have to approach your child and get the conversation started. So go ahead. Not so easy, right? As trained professionals, we sometimes find it a little awkward and uncomfortable to talk to children or adolescents about their self-injury, so we can only imagine how hard it must be for a parent to approach a self-injuring child. The goal of this chapter is to set you up with an arsenal of tools to utilize in the event that your child is not enthusiastic about talking to you about cutting (which, if you ask us, is pretty likely).

Realize that, by reading this book, you're already more prepared than the average parent of a self-injuring child. You have a whole lot of knowledge and skills that don't come in the parent handbook. What? You didn't get the parent handbook? I'm so sorry. But don't worry—there wasn't a chapter on cutting in it anyway.

HOW TO START A DIALOGUE

The initial dialogue may seem like the most daunting one to have with your child. You may be concerned about how you will address the issue and persuade him to seek treatment if your child shuts down after your first talk. You're not sure how he will respond, since this is new territory for you. The key is to approach the task with a little bit of planning and a lot of confidence in your ability to demonstrate both your knowledge of self-injury and your desire to help your child.

Picking a Good Time

There is no right time to approach your child about self-injury, but there are certainly some times that might affect your chances of success. In fact, determining when such a conversation would be less likely to succeed will guide you to choose a time when it could be successful. Some not-so-great times to approach your child about cutting include the following: in front of friends, siblings, or family members; while at a recreational event; during an existing argument; in a public place; or while you or your child is busy, under stress, or distracted.

Barring any of these circumstances, there's no wrong time for the cutting conversation to occur. However, it's probably better if you pick a time when neither of you is under time pressure (for example, have your talk when you've settled in for the evening rather than when you're running off to work in the morning), when you are rested and focused, and when you don't have to compete with other, possibly cooler or more interesting, stimuli (TV, friends, computer, phone, and so on). Picking a private place where you both feel comfortable and can speak freely is also helpful. You may want to ask your child if he would like to talk in his room.

Make Your Words Count

In addition, some useful hints can help steer your conversation toward a strong dialogue in which both you and your child are invested, actively participating, and sharing in the conversation. Generally, it's helpful to have a game plan going in, so you can stay on track. Some people need to write things down and some feel more comfortable just bulleting certain points in their heads. Know your style and stick with it. Don't worry about how it looks, whether you're referring to notes you've written on an index card or just remembering the points in your head—if it helps you to stay calm and on point, it's a good strategy.

If your child is like most teenagers, you have exactly thirty seconds to make your point before he's turned off, bored, or wondering exactly what it is that you're really trying to say. Say what you mean, and mean what you say. Right off the bat, let your child know that you love him, that you're concerned (and why), that you think he might be self-injuring (and why), and that you want to talk about it.

If it helps, you might want to acknowledge your own discomfort and your child's too. It's not every day that you two sit down and have a heart-to-heart about the razor blade you found in his jeans pocket, or the scarred skin you glimpsed beneath his sleeve while he was doing dishes. Regardless, convey that as uncomfortable as it may be for both of you, you are committed to talking about this.

If you can't imagine what would ever make someone want to hurt themselves, then it's okay to say that, along with the message that you've been doing some reading and you now understand much better why some people use self-injury to cope with negative feelings or events. The most important thing is to be genuine. Your concern is so real and so palpable that you probably feel like it's weighing you down, and your child will likely perceive this. Trying to play it off as if you're just curious or just seeking information would be untruthful. So be willing to lay your cards on the table, because, in essence, you're asking your child to do the same.

HOW TO DIRECTLY ASK ABOUT SELF-INJURY

Asking your child about his cutting will probably be one of the hardest questions you ask as a parent. However, imagine how this conversation feels for your child. You'll see that having to answer a parent honestly when you have been hurting yourself is probably one of the hardest things your adolescent will go through. Things could get heated, but hopefully your candor and focus will keep your interaction from getting hostile. If you find that your child's response to your asking about his hurting himself is a hostile one, this isn't an admission of guilt, nor is it indicative of anything except anger at being asked this question. You can quickly defuse the conflict by validating his feelings and stating how annoyed you'd be if someone asked you such a question (and you probably would be). Then restate why you're concerned and why you're asking.

By validating your child's feelings of anger and discomfort, you're keeping the focus on his feelings. You're helping to demonstrate that this really is about him, not about you (the conversation would be about you if you went on a rant about how disappointed, angry, and afraid you were). This could also help you to stay focused. If you remind yourself before you begin that you're having this incredibly hard and weird conversation not for you but for your child, who seems to be in trouble, you may find that you want to avoid the whole topic a little less.

In order to encourage a dialogue instead of restaging the Spanish Inquisition, try asking open-ended questions and using a nonaccusatory tone. Of course, you knew that, but in the heat of such a conversation, it's really easy to forget. This is especially the case when your teen turns the tables on you (sometimes in order to deflect the focus away from him) by saying something like "Why do you think that? Have you been going through my things? God, I have no privacy!" or "I can't believe you would even ask me that! What's wrong with you? Do you really think I'd do something weird like that?"

Remember, you don't have to defend yourself here, nor do you have to pin your teen to the mat. This conversation is happening because you're a loving, concerned parent who has reason to believe that the child that you love is in tremendous emotional distress and may be injuring himself. So, a good open-ended way to ask about cutting would be to say, "I notice that you've been really struggling lately. You seem so sad [or "angry," or another feeling]. I really care about you and I want to help. You may think it's strange for me to say this, but I'm worried that you might be hurting yourself or thinking about it. What do you think and feel about what I just said?"

By asking this way, you're not posing a yes-or-no question to your child but are instead opening up the floor to him and allowing him the freedom to really talk to you about his feelings, experiences, and behaviors. At least it might get him to say a little more than just a single syllable. Also, it allows you room to state that you don't perceive cutting as the only or most important problem, but as part of the whole picture. In essence, the conversation designed to address cutting winds up focusing on your child and his difficulties and also on your concern and willingness to be there for him.

It's important to remember, however, that in this conversation you are trying to gather information about your child's dangerous behavior. Therefore, do find a way to ask the following questions:

- How long have you been cutting?

- How often do you cut?

- Where on your body do you cut?

- What motivates you to cut?

- Have you tried to stop?

- What happened when you tried to stop?

By getting accurate answers to these questions, you are doing a brief assessment of your child's cutting behavior that will allow you to evaluate what type of help is necessary (such as outpatient therapy or immediate hospitalization). Again, these questions will help you stay focused on your child and his behavior, without getting sidetracked by your feelings and thoughts about the cutting. Of course, you're probably curious about where your child learned this behavior, and what you've done as a parent that either encouraged or discouraged cutting, but try to hold off on those questions, because they don't really help you or your child right away. They'll be more valuable later on, once the problem is being addressed.

Now that you have crossed the most difficult hurdle, that first conversation, you may believe that you have accomplished only a small part of the larger task at hand (more so if your child's response was less than ideal): helping your child to stop cutting. But, despite his reaction, you have in fact communicated two valuable messages to your child already: that you are knowledgeable about self-injury and that you are invested in helping him overcome his struggles in a compassionate and caring manner.

6

Responding to Answers: Common Obstacles to Communication About Self-Injury

We hope that the previous chapter provided you with some concrete skills to use when starting productive conversations with your child regarding her self-injurious behavior. This chapter is designed to help you handle your child's responses if they are less than positive. We hope that your first conversation went exceedingly well, but we will be honest: you will probably encounter some roadblocks along the way. We know that communicating your genuine concern in a nonthreatening, supportive, and calm manner can be quite challenging due to the difficult nature of the topic. Your child may not want to have this conversation with you at all. Consequently, you may encounter some very unpredictable responses, including hostility, anger, denial, excuses, and even the silent treatment. We urge you to hang in there, and be patient yet persistent.

In this chapter we'll discuss the most common situations that parents encounter when confronting their children about self-injury.

HELP! My Child Refuses to Talk About It

So you used all of our guidelines for getting a conversation started, and your child responded by looking directly at you and saying that she didn't know what you were talking about because she has *not* been cutting. Instead, she insisted that you are the one with the problem and accused you of either being too nosy, watching too many talk shows, or reading too many self-help books.

In order to foster a productive and healing conversation with your child, follow the guidelines below:

1. Start out by validating your child's emotions and point of view. This means acknowledging how difficult this may be for her.

2. Describe the behaviors you have observed that make you suspect she may be self-injuring. This is a crucial step in the process. Expressing the facts to your child in a clear and unemotional manner will help you strengthen your case. Be as specific and detailed as you can. Stick to evidence that you have direct knowledge of and behaviors that you have observed. It is best to stay away from giving opinions and stating suspicions for which you have no concrete evidence at the moment. For example, don't accuse your child of cutting all day in school or doing this for years if you don't have the evidence to back up your statement.

3. Express your care and concern.

4. Gently encourage your child to discuss the topic with you.

5. Reassure your child about the consequences of admitting to the behavior. Remind your child that you will not be angry, and that she will not be kicked out of the house or punished

in any other way. State that you simply want to help. Most people are reluctant to admit something if they fear some negative consequences for their actions. You don't want your child to feel that she is being backed into a corner with no way out.

Now, if you're wondering how to actually communicate all of the above points, here is a step-by-step example of the kinds of things you can say to your child:

1. **Validate:** "I understand that it can be very annoying to be asked about such a difficult and personal topic. I can guess that you may be very uncomfortable, scared, or even angry talking to me about this."

2. **Describe the behavior:** "I have noticed a change in your behavior in the past two months. You seem so unhappy and angry lately. You've spent less time doing things you enjoy, like basketball and piano. You refused to go to your pediatrician's appointment last week, which never seemed to bother you before. You have spent more time alone, away from your family. For the last two weeks, you have eaten in your room rather than at your usual spot at the kitchen table with us. I also notice some marks on your arms and found some tissues with blood on your bathroom counter. All of these things together make me suspect that you may be hurting yourself."

3. **Express your care and concern:** "I love you and am very concerned about you. It seems like you are going through a difficult time and I want to help."

4. **Encourage a conversation:** "Can you tell me about what has been going on in the past two months?"

5. **Tell your child what to expect:** "I know that this is not your fault and I will not be upset at you if you tell me what's been happening. I will do my best to remain understanding and supportive of you. I still love you no matter what you tell me. I don't have all the answers, but if you talk to me about this, I can find a way to help you."

If your child responds by admitting that she has been cutting, stay calm and supportive, as you have promised. Just continue to encourage her to talk so that you can accumulate enough necessary information to decide which course of action to take. Try to keep your questions to a minimum and allow her to express herself. If you believe your child is minimizing the amount or severity of cutting she engages in, this is not the time to challenge her on the facts. This will just frustrate her and cause her to end the conversation prematurely. Just keep validating her feelings by expressing your concern, acknowledging how difficult it must be to discuss this, and telling her how proud you are of her maturity for deciding to engage in this discussion. As long as your child admits that she is having a problem, then the details are not as important as the admission in the immediate moment. If she is curious and is looking for some information about what she's been going through, answer her questions to the best of your ability. Tell her what you have learned about self-injury from reading this book and any other materials you've consulted. Remind her that she is not to blame. End the conversation by offering to provide her with some information you have gathered via the Internet, books, and other media so she can learn more about self-injury independently. Tell her that you will look into finding some professionals who can help her, as well as teach the family how to support her while she overcomes this behavior. Acknowledge that seeking help is scary and hard work but that you are confident in her ability to persevere. Reiterate your pride about her courage and willingness to engage in this conversation with you.

HELP! Should I Believe My Child When She Promises to Stop?

So you had a conversation with your child regarding the self-injury and she was willing to admit that she has been cutting for the last few months. She acknowledged the behavior but minimized or dismissed it. She tells you that it's no big deal; she can stop any time she wants and doesn't require treatment. She seems quite sincere in her promise to stop. Parents often struggle with whether to give their child some degree of freedom or listen to their intuition. If your gut instinct warns you that she may not be able to fulfill her promise despite the best intentions, how do you actually communicate this to her without jeopardizing your relationship?

We suggest that you start by praising your child for her honesty and her willingness to change. Then provide your child with some of the facts you have learned about self-injury, specifically that it can quickly become an addictive behavior and that it is very difficult to just stop without the guidance and knowledge of an expert. If she insists that she wants to try on her own, then you may have to give her a couple of chances to stop. Attempt to compromise on a concrete agreement that specifies an amount of time in which she will try to stop and that stipulates that she will agree to seek help if she continues to struggle.

Collecting some basic information about the cutting itself is crucial when you're dealing with your child's denials, excuses, and/or promises. All of the recommendations in the remainder of this chapter apply in low-risk situations, meaning that the cutting is not placing your child in immediate risk for accidental serious injury or death. If your child is dissociating while she is cutting, if she is taking increased risks in other areas of life (such as driving recklessly, refusing to wear her seatbelt, and so on), or is using drugs or alcohol when she cuts, then delaying treatment is not worth the risk. In addition, if she refuses to tell you about her behavior or you learn that the cuts have become deeper or that she is cutting in a potentially dangerous location on her body, then take action. If you don't have sufficient information or are not confident in your ability to determine whether the self-injury is increasingly dangerous and requires immediate attention, then at some point you'll need to use your authority as parent and step in despite what the child does or does not agree to do. Make an immediate appointment with a psychologist or, if your child is in immediate danger, seek out hospitalization. Otherwise, some negotiation in the short term may be necessary in order to give your child some perception of control over the situation so that she will eventually agree to treatment on her own terms. Therapy goes much more smoothly with a willing patient.

Here are some suggestions for how to have this type of discussion with your child:

Parent: I'm so proud of you for discussing this with me. I know it must be difficult to talk about this. I'm also so glad to hear that you are willing to stop cutting. To be honest with you, though, I am a bit concerned about you trying to stop on your own. From all the research and books I've read, I gather that this is not something people just started doing out of choice. You must be really struggling with so much right now. A therapist trained in helping people with self-injury could help you in an effective way. From what I've learned so far in researching self-injury, it sounds like you would learn some concrete skills and strategies you can use when you are having urges to cut.

Child: Mom, I want you to trust me. I know other kids may need therapy. I don't. I haven't been cutting for that long and I know I can stop. Why won't you believe me? Just give me a chance. I know I can do this.

Parent: It sounds like you are willing to try really hard and would like me to give you the benefit of the doubt. I can agree to give you some time, even though I am uncomfortable with your decision. Let's discuss this in a little more detail so together we can decide on a plan that works. Tell me a little bit about the cutting. How often are you doing it? Where on your body have you been cutting? How long have you been cutting? What kinds of situations trigger the urge to cut? Have you ever tried to stop before?

Child: Oh, Mom, why do you have to know all this? This is none of your business!

Parent: I can imagine that from your perspective this seems like private information that you don't feel like discussing. I am willing to give you some space in the future, but for right now I need some information so that we can do what's in your best interest. I am concerned about your physical safety and am asking these questions to make sure that you are not putting yourself at risk.

Once your child gives you some information and you determine that giving her some time is the best course of action, then negotiate a reasonable time in which she can try to stop on her own.

Parent: Can we come to an agreement to give you some time to try to stop cutting? If you are still struggling after that time, I would like you to discuss it with me so we can take the next step. When do you think we should have this discussion again?

Child: How about in a month?

Parent: I'd feel more comfortable if we discussed it again in two weeks and then we can just take it from there.

HELP! My Child Is Still Refusing to Talk

If your child still won't admit that she has been cutting despite your efforts to discuss your concerns with her, then it may be helpful to back off for a few days. Inform your child that you respect her privacy and will give her some time to think things over, but tell her that you intend to pursue this conversation again at a later date. Giving your child some control over the situation and some degree of privacy will help decrease the power struggle between the two of you.

If you think that your child will not discuss this with you but would agree to speak confidentially to a mental health professional, then by all means offer that solution instead. Communicate to your child that the most important thing is that she gets the proper help. The goal is not for you to learn all the details of her difficulties at the current moment, but rather to gather sufficient information in order to pursue the most appropriate treatment. We have found that this approach can work quite well, especially if you explain the concept of therapist-client confidentiality. Once your child enters treatment, the therapist can take the responsibility for describing the limits of confidentiality. The therapist can then help you, your child, and your family members to develop concrete guidelines regarding what will be shared with you and what will be kept confidential between your child and her therapist. Rest assured that all therapists are legally and ethically bound to break confidentiality if they believe that the child is an imminent risk to herself and/or others. Once your child enters treatment, talk with the therapist about this legal requirement; having this knowledge will give you some degree of comfort and the ability to step back if your child requests it. Self-injury by definition would seem to be a cause to break the client-therapist confidentiality, but the therapist will assess the degree of danger your child is in based on many factors, including the location, tools, and method of cutting. If the therapist notices that your child's behavior is becoming increasingly dangerous, then you will certainly become involved in an immediate plan to decrease the degree of risk, possibly including hospitalization.

Here are some suggestions for what to say to your child if she continues to resist having a conversation with you:

Parent:　I understand that you may still be struggling with the decision to speak to me right now, but I would like to speak with you about this when you are ready. Can we discuss this in a few days?

Child:　No way!

Parent:　I respect your need for privacy but I am concerned about you and love you. I will do my best not to bring this up until next week and to allow you some time to think. If you want to talk sooner, then I will make my best effort to be understanding and listen. In the meantime, here are some things I gathered from the Internet in my own search to learn more about self-injury.

Child:　Mom, you are so wrong. I am not cutting and I refuse to talk to you about it. I don't care how many times you ask me, I will not respond.

Parent:　I know that parents can be wrong sometimes. But even if you are not cutting, I am still concerned about you because I have noticed a change in your behavior and your mood lately. And I still don't know why you have been hiding your arms and refusing to go to the doctor. All of these things make me believe that something is wrong. Even if it's something else, I'd like to find a way to help you.

Child: You couldn't possibly help me!

Parent: Maybe I couldn't. I understand that you might not want to talk to me about this. Would you be willing to speak to a professional who could help you? If you do, I will give you my word to back off and let you have a confidential discussion with the professional. You don't even have to tell me what you discuss with this person.

Once you have given your word that you will not bring up self-injury for a week, then it is important for you to keep your word and stay away from the topic unless your child approaches you first. You may have to continue these kinds of conversations with your child on a regular basis until she opens up and discusses things with you.

We know that parents become so frustrated and worried that they sometimes find themselves resorting to indirect methods in an attempt to get their child to admit their behavior, but we don't find that this is useful in the long run. It will jeopardize your ability to develop a trusting relationship with your child, one in which you are able to have conversations about the self-injury. Setting up a situation that fosters healthy communication will allow you to stay involved in her progress, which can be a valuable asset once your child is in treatment. Under the right circumstances, parents and close family can be an integral part of a person's recovery from any mental illness (not just self-injury). As clinicians, we work with family members to help include them as part of a supportive team and to become "therapeutic coaches." This means that if your child struggles with the strategies she learns in therapy, she can seek your coaching between therapy sessions rather than just giving in to the urge to cut. Building a trusting and safe relationship between you will help your child in the long run, even if that means having to back down from these initial conversations. It is an important goal to keep in sight. In future chapters, we will help you learn techniques you can use with your child once she is in treatment that will help you support her recovery.

HELP! My Child Is Finding Excuses!

It would not surprise us if you tried to have a couple of conversations with your child and she responded by making excuses, giving rational explanations, or minimizing the situation rather than simply denying the behavior. You followed our step-by-step guidelines and provided your child with a list of behaviors you have observed, and she came up with explanations such as "I fell in gym class," "The cat scratched me," or "I don't know how I did it. Maybe I cut myself on the school locker or during art class." Your child might have even given reasons why her mood or behavior has changed, such as "God, Mom, I've just been stressed over school lately. Don't make such a big deal out of it!"

So how should you respond to these kinds of scenarios? Just keep in mind that your child is probably not deliberately trying to make your life more difficult. She is genuinely suffering and may be terribly afraid about what will happen if she opens up to you. In these circumstances, just use the same steps as you would if your child were denying the behavior completely. Reiterate what you have observed, express your concern, but let her know that you will try to have this conversation again at a later date. If you have written material, give it to her.

Some children even respond, "So what if I've been cutting? Lots of kids at school are doing it and their parents aren't getting this worked up about it." And your child is probably correct. She may in fact know other kids who are engaging in the behavior! In this case, acknowledge that although this has become a more common problem in recent years, you take it seriously and know that it requires some action. Acknowledge that every parent has his or her own way of handling things, but that you believe that the best course of action is to provide your child with the best possible help when she is going through a difficult time. You don't believe in ignoring or denying problems. If something is upsetting any member of your family, then you believe in acknowledging and working through the problem.

If you don't seem to be making progress after a few attempted conversations, then it is probably better to stop trying for a little while. Attempting to engage your child in a conversation too frequently will probably backfire. We suggest that you consider other alternatives, such as seeking a few sessions of mental health treatment for yourself in order to find out how to guide your child toward treatment. Find a professional who is very familiar with self-injury, so that he or she can provide you with some concrete feedback and suggestions on how to interact with your child. Take the opportunity to also collect as much information about self-injury and its treatment as you can. Receiving some support for yourself during this very stressful time has its own obvious benefits, too. If your child won't see a professional, then maybe you can begin to implement some of the provider's recommended therapeutic techniques with your child until she does accept treatment. We don't suggest that you take the role of therapist, which could certainly affect your relationship with your child, but introducing your child to some of the concepts might increase her motivation to agree to treatment.

The suggestions we have provided in this chapter have worked for a majority of the parents we have worked with. We hope they will work for you!

In the next chapter we will introduce you to the most effective psychological therapy for treating self-injury. At this point you have gained the skills to get your child to that first therapy appointment. Now it's essential to make sure that she will receive the most appropriate help available.

7

Psychological Treatment Options

We often throw around the word "help" as a generic reference to counseling or something related to psychiatric services (as in "You need *help*!"). However, "help" can run the gamut from pastoral counseling or talking to a school guidance counselor to seeking out a psychiatric consultation or hospitalization. If you're at the point where you have resolved to enlist the aid of professionals and are discussing getting professional assistance for your child, you've obviously accepted and gotten him to accept the fact that his self-injury is not only a problematic behavior but also an expression of his painful emotional experiences. Stop for a second and pat yourself on the back. You've made it through the hardest part of the process of dealing with your child's self-injury (and we know it's *all* hard).

You may have just saved your child's life in more ways than one. This is a big deal! However, we can almost guarantee that you're more anxious now than you were before you addressed your child's cutting. Rather than breathing a sigh of relief, you're probably sweating bullets, hoping you can find the right kind of treatment to really help your child. This can seem like such a daunting task. We understand your worry, because by the time many families make it to us they've been seeking help for some time and are often frustrated about some of the advice they've gotten.

One teenage girl we treated, who was highly motivated to get help for her cutting, had sought advice from her school guidance counselor, who sent her to the school psychologist, who told her that she was suicidal (though she clearly was not), called her mother and told her to take her daughter to an adolescent psychiatric unit, where she was admitted, told she was just being melodramatic and seeking attention, and released to the care of a social worker, who advised the girl to snap a rubber band around her wrist and call a friend if she felt like cutting (which, by the way, did not work). This intentional run-on sentence illustrates this family's very frustrating experience, which would be correctly termed the "runaround." In order to help you avoid getting the runaround, we have compiled some guidelines for getting the right kind of help immediately.

THE RIGHT KIND OF HELP

You are now at the point in addressing your child's self-injury and related emotional distress where you need to involve an expert. You need someone who can work with both you and your child in order to identify exactly what issues are triggering the self-injury, provide effective treatment strategies, and, most important, help your child heal physically and emotionally. But even among "experts," the right training and approach to self-injury can make all the difference in your child's recovery.

The first step to finding the right resources is to understand the differences in terminology and qualifications among the professionals. Identifying the right professional can prove to be an exceptionally confusing process, since there are so many people out there claiming that they have all the answers. Nobody really has *all* the answers, but finding someone who is properly trained to help your child may mean that you get more of the answers, and some good advice too.

Below is a quick guide to the differences in titles, functions, and qualifications among those in the mental health field. We have included a variety of treatment professionals; however, our list is definitely not exhaustive. We're almost positive you'll come up with some options we've left out. However, this list contains descriptions of the types of professionals that you're likely to come in contact with in your quest for help.

Psychiatrists

Psychiatrists are medical doctors who are trained to prescribe psychotropic medication. Though they may have training in therapeutic techniques, they are currently more prescription oriented and their training is more classically psychoanalytic (think true Freudian couch therapy). Many psychiatrists may also be psychopharmacologists (see below) but not refer to themselves in that way. Psychiatrists may be valuable in prescribing medications, if needed, which would be determined by the professional providing the therapy.

Psychopharmacologists

Medical doctors who specialize in prescribing psychotropic medications, psychopharmacologists share many functions with psychiatrists but are generally medication specialists and tend not to do actual therapy. They may be a valuable source for prescribed medications if needed, but that need would be determined by the professional providing the therapy.

Psychologists

Psychologists may be either Ph.D.'s (having earned a doctorate of philosophy in psychology, which entails four to five years of graduate training) or Psy.D.'s (having earned a doctorate of applied psychology, which entails approximately the same amount of graduate training). Both are trained in the assessment, diagnosis, and treatment of psychological disorders. They are also trained to do psychometric testing. These are the highest degrees in the field among those who are specifically trained to do hands-on treatment. Psychologists can, however, differ significantly in their training. We recommend seeking out a psychologist trained in cognitive behavioral therapy (CBT) or a variant of CBT called dialectical behavior therapy (DBT). Even if psychologists say they know how to do CBT or DBT, make sure you ask specifically what they would do for your child, and make up your mind accordingly.

Master's Level Psychologists

Master's level psychologists, who may also refer to themselves simply as "psychologists," have either an MA (master of arts) or an MS (master of science) degree, both which require approximately two years of graduate training. These professionals are trained in psychological assessment, treatment, and psychometric testing. Master's level psychologists may do independent hands-on therapy but are generally supervised by doctoral level psychologists. They may do many of the same things as doctoral level psychologists; the distinction is simply based on the discrepancy in their level of graduate training. Again, look for individuals trained in CBT or DBT.

Social Workers

Social workers, MSWs (a title that requires a master's degree in social work and two years of graduate training) and CSWs (clinical social workers, who also have master's degrees but are more clinically oriented), may provide therapy, but they do so generally at a community level (at locations such as mental health centers and clinics) or in group or family therapy capacities. Some individuals have doctorates in social work, but this is significantly less common. Social workers are less often oriented toward cognitive behavioral therapy and are more often trained in supportive, systemic (how the behavior functions for the individual in the family setting, for example), and analytically based (Freudian) therapies. You may find the occasional social worker with training in CBT or DBT, but most will have a different theoretical orientation.

Counselors

Counselors have master's degrees (MAs) in counseling and may be found in such positions as school guidance counselor. These individuals are trained to spot problems when they occur and to give general advice, not to administer the specific types of therapy we have been discussing. Counselors are also trained to make appropriate referrals for specific issues.

ASKING THE RIGHT QUESTIONS

So now you know exactly what the specific titles and letters after people's names imply, and what type of training is preferable (we'll discuss the reasons behind our training recommendations shortly). At this point, we very strongly urge you to think about interviewing several professionals before you make an appointment. If your roof were in need of repair, you'd probably do some research about the roofing companies in your area before you chose one, perhaps calling the Better Business Bureau or licensing board, asking for referrals, and so on. Well, we know you value your children far more than your roof, so we encourage you to give the process of selecting a treatment professional the same due diligence.

We know that it might be intimidating to interview professionals when you are feeling overwhelmed, frightened, angry, guilty, or helpless. However, keep in mind that while they may be experts at administering specific treatments, you are the expert on your child. Don't be shy about asking the same kinds of questions you would ask potential roofers. Though the letters after their name will give you a pretty good idea of their level of training, don't hesitate to ask if you're unclear about it. Below is a list of some basic questions to start with when you are looking into treatment professionals. We encourage you to come up with some questions of your own, too.

- What is your theoretical orientation? (Remember, you are looking for training in cognitive behavioral therapy or dialectical behavior therapy.)

- Do you have experience treating self-injury?

- Do you have experience treating adolescents (or children)?

- Are you affiliated with any hospitals?

- Are you licensed? (If the individual is still in training, ask about how and by whom he or she is supervised.)

- What other classes of disorders do you treat? (This is a particularly important question, because we've already established that self-injury is often a symptom of, or at least co-occurs with, other disorders [such as mood, anxiety, personality, eating, and body-image disorders].)

- Do you feel comfortable working with parents as well as their children to help implement the appropriate strategies at home?

- Will you work with the school, pediatrician, psychiatrist, and any other institutions and individuals in my child's life to provide comprehensive treatment?

If a treatment professional is not receptive to being interviewed briefly before your consultation appointment, or if you are uncomfortable with the person's answers to your questions, keep looking! The search can be a daunting process, but the right professionals can make all the difference in your child's treatment.

Another factor to consider is whether your child would prefer a treatment professional of one gender or the other. This issue may seem inconsequential, but trust us—it really counts to some kids. It can be a particularly big deal for children who have been sexually abused or have body-image disturbance, social anxiety, or an eating disorder. Ask your child if he has a preference, and then do your best to find a well-qualified individual of that gender. It is important that your child be able to relate to and feel comfortable with his treatment professionals. Good rapport and a reasonable level of comfort can help to establish a solid groundwork for good therapy.

COGNITIVE BEHAVIORAL THERAPY AND DIALECTICAL BEHAVIOR THERAPY

Have we mentioned these treatment modalities yet? Oh, only throughout the whole book. Why are we harping on these therapeutic orientations? Wouldn't anyone with a kind ear be helpful in a crisis situation? No. We can't express clearly enough that these are the treatments of choice when dealing with self-injury and the related psychological issues. Why? Research demonstrates that they actually work. Enough said.

Let's talk about what CBT and DBT are and why they work. Have you ever been in a really low mood, when everything in life just seemed to be going wrong, and you felt fat, dumb, ugly, and like the Bad Luck Fairy stuffed her magic wand up your nose? Okay, so then you know that when you're feeling that way you tend to view things in a very negative light, and sometimes, when your mood changes to a more positive state, you realize exactly how off base your perception was. Adolescence can be considered the temporary state of existence defined by self-consciousness, lack of self-confidence, moodiness, and the tendency to view things through a more negative filter. Now, add to that debilitating depression, severe anxiety, or loathing of one's own body and imagine how skewed your perceptions (and your feelings and behaviors) would be.

Faulty or irrational thinking is associated with negative emotional experiences and behaviors. Often, when someone is experiencing a high level of emotional distress, they begin to view life from a much more negative perspective—the opposite of rose-colored glasses. All of their sensory input comes through a dark, bleak, depressing filter (sometimes we refer to this filter as "crap-colored glasses").

A sixteen-year-old girl whose depression was alleviated after about six months stated, "It was like being trapped in a fun house, except it was the opposite of fun. I saw myself distorted and disfigured everywhere I turned. Half the time, I couldn't recognize myself or my thoughts anymore. I would feel so negative, and then I would act so negative. I would be thinking, 'Everyone hates me' or 'Nobody talks to me because I'm so ugly and stupid,' so I would act so cold and withdrawn. Then when they stayed away, I'd say, 'See, it's because they hate me and because I suck so much.' I was trapped in a vicious cycle and I couldn't get out of it. Cutting was my only escape."

Cognitive Behavioral Therapy

Cognitive behavioral therapy is a two-pronged approach that targets both the faulty (negative, rigid, or distorted) thought patterns, or cognitions, and the maladaptive behaviors (avoidance, isolation, compulsions, self-injury) that created the negative loop that our patient described above. Our thoughts influence our feelings, which influence our behaviors. You don't necessarily get to choose how you feel, especially if you are in the midst of a biologically based problem, but you can learn to think more flexibly or adaptively. And you can engage in behaviors that either help to disconfirm your faulty thinking or are simply healthier.

Here's an example of how we would challenge some faulty thinking in an actual session:

Patient: I'm a total failure. Everything I do I screw up and I let everyone down all the time. I wish I were dead.

Therapist: It sounds like things seem pretty messed up for you right now. I'm not arguing with you, but those are pretty extreme statements. I don't think I've ever met anyone who was a *total* failure. Maybe you're being too hard on yourself. Is there anything, today for example, that you didn't screw up?

Patient: That's not what I mean. Of course I don't screw everything up . . .

Therapist: So, what did you do right today?

Patient: I did do well on a test, but that doesn't fix anything.

Therapist: It doesn't fix anything, but saying you're a total failure is really unfair to yourself. Not to mention inaccurate. We all make mistakes.

Patient: That's so played out. I know, now you're going to give me the "I'm okay, you're okay" speech. Ugh!

Therapist: Okay, so I won't. I'm just going to remind you that you are a member of the human race and the rules that apply to the rest of us mere mortals apply to you too.

I didn't realize that you were being held to a higher standard than the rest of us.

Patient: I set high standards for myself. If I don't, I'll be a total failure.

Therapist: Wait, I thought you were a total failure. Well, not a total failure, I guess, but a partial failure like the rest of us. That also means you're a partial success. Which means there's no way that you suck as badly as you might think you do.

I have no problem with high standards. But there's high, which is good—they help you achieve—and then there's *high,* as in unrealistically, relentlessly, perfectionistically high. These standards only set you up for failure. You can never be satisfied with what you do, because no matter what, nothing's ever good enough.

Patient: Well, nothing ever is.

Therapist: Nothing? You haven't done anything you're proud of or that you like?

Patient: Okay, I'm a good artist. I have one picture I like a lot, but that doesn't count.

Therapist: Why?

Patient: Because it's just art.

Therapist: I'm sorry. I'll contact Picasso on the Ouija board and let him know he's also an insignificant failure.

Patient: Whatever. I still let everyone down all the time.

Therapist: You have never let me down.

Patient: You don't count.

Therapist: Oh, right. Everyone except me . . . and your parents.

Patient: I let them down.

Therapist: Of course you do sometimes. Haven't they ever let you down?

Patient: Yeah, I guess.

Therapist: Okay, so you've given them a little slack. Could you try to extend the same courtesy to yourself?

Patient: Okay, I get your point. Nobody's perfect and I'm being too hard on myself. I still feel lousy.

Therapist: Lousy we can deal with; that's different from wanting to die.

You can see from the dialogue how the therapist used logic to challenge the negative, irrational beliefs in order to help the patient adopt a more moderate, adaptive viewpoint. The goal of the therapeutic process is to ferret out extreme, rigid thinking—the same thinking that contributes to negative emotional experiences and behaviors—and to modify it. The process takes time, but it can be effective when combined with behavioral modification techniques.

We know—"behavior modification" sounds so *Clockwork Orange*. However, it's a highly useful therapy that helps an individual identify maladaptive behaviors and figure out how to change them. It's actually very effective (especially when used in combination with cognitive therapy) at treating anxiety disorders like obsessive-compulsive disorder, as well as eating disorders, body dysmorphic disorder, and other compulsive behaviors.

The theory on which behavior modification is based is that individuals who engage in repetitive maladaptive behaviors, regardless of the specific behavior, are routinely reinforced for doing them in some particular way. If we can help identify how the person is being reinforced and then have the person resist the problem behavior, we can break the cycle.

As an example, we'll use the case of Karyn, a fifteen-year-old who has an eating disorder (not quite anorexia, but getting there) and self-injures. When Karyn perceives herself as fat, she either engages in compensatory exercise until she views herself as thinner, or she self-injures to punish herself for her perceived transgression. By engaging in these behaviors, she reports that she is able to experience relief, the feeling of being "cleansed," and achieve a sense of control over her own body. One problem with this cycle is that her unhealthy beliefs are strengthened, because they are validated every time she behaves as if they are true. The other problem is that her compulsive exercise and cutting have become habitual, because they provide Karyn with a sense of control and relief.

To address Karyn's eating disorder and self-injury behaviorally, we would construct a list of discomfort-provoking thoughts, feelings, behaviors, and situations that Karyn would then place in order from least to most uncomfortable (for example, eating some of her "off-limits" foods, wearing a swimsuit, wearing anything other than a baggy sweatshirt in front of a guy she really likes). Then we would start with some of the lower items on her hierarchy and have her do some of these uncomfortable things while we helped her resist engaging in compensatory exercise or cutting. The purpose of having her do things that make her uncomfortable and then preventing her from engaging in her "comforting" behavior is to allow her to feel her fears long enough to experience the natural reduction in discomfort that occurs with time.

There are individuals who practice cognitive or behavioral therapy alone, but in combination they really provide the one-two punch necessary for helping your child overcome self-injury and the related issues. We would recommend someone who practices cognitive *and* behavioral therapy over someone who practices cognitive therapy alone, especially for obsessional thinking, compulsive behaviors, and depression.

Dialectical Behavior Therapy

Dialectical behavior therapy, developed by Marsha Linehan (1993a), is a variation of standard cognitive behavioral therapy that has shown success in helping individuals who are chronically suicidal, self-injurious, and have significant problems with mood regulation (such as individuals with borderline personality disorder and post-traumatic stress disorder). While this modality also focuses on learning more adaptive thinking styles and on practicing healthier and less emotion-driven behaviors, it has some additional elements that lend themselves particularly well to treating those with mood lability, poor tolerance for negative emotions, problems with interpersonal interactions, chronic suicidality, and self-injurious behavior.

The word dialectic implies finding a balance between the reality of the individual (which may be skewed as a result of faulty perceptions due to psychological disturbance) and the direct opposite of his perspective (Linehan 1993a). The goal of this type of therapy is to teach the individual to view things from a less polarized or extreme perspective, which will eventually enable him to take into account the whole picture, value other positions, and gain a more balanced perspective.

It can be a little tough to wrap your brain around this concept, so we sometimes explain it with this adage: "There are three sides to every story: your side, their side, and the truth." Dialectical behavior therapy helps individuals work on seeking the "truth," and, in doing so, helps to reduce harmful, emotion-driven behaviors. The following are some key skills targeted in DBT (Linehan 1993b):

- Regulating emotions through engaging in certain behaviors (self-soothing and mood improvement measures, for example) and thinking patterns

- Improving one's ability to handle distress and discomfort by learning specific patterns of coping with negative emotions and situations

- Helping the individual remain in the here and now using core mindfulness strategies, instead of dwelling on past regrets or future anxieties; also allows individuals to be less entangled in intense negative emotions

- Learning the skills to function more effectively in the context of social relationships and interpersonal interactions (for example, learning how to be more appropriately assertive, and how to address and handle conflict)

■ Anne's Story

Anne, one of our patients, fondly refers to her DBT training as "the point at which I learned to get off the speeding freight train of emotions, where I was always telling everyone else where to get off, or blaming them for my lousy trip." She added, "I actually started dealing with my life and my problems in a responsible way."

As part of her treatment, she was asked to begin taking responsibility for her own actions, including her self-injury. One of the ways we accomplished this was to have her really examine how her pattern of self-injury was related to uncomfortable interactions with specific people who were close to her (for example, her parents, sister, friends, teachers, and coaches). At first, she really struggled with this, stating that she self-injured for no particular reason and that there was no message she was trying to send. She simply blamed others for her cutting: "My mom was such a bitch today. She just kept going on and on about how I have to do better in school. I told her I couldn't take it and she just wouldn't shut up. So I cut myself. When she started to get on my case about that too, I said, 'Are you happy now? Look what you made me do! I hate you, I hate myself, and I hate my life!'"

An adapted DBT technique that proved to be particularly useful for this patient was what we refer to as "breaking it down" (we will discuss this technique in more detail in chapter 10). Essentially, by having her record some specific information about her episodes of self-injury, we were able to collaboratively arrive at some recurring themes in Anne's cutting. First, we approached each episode of self-injury as distinct, assuming that it had nothing in common with any previous incident. Then, we began to break it down by trying to identify what preceded it. Using the above example, we might identify a few triggers: (1) Anne was very sensitive about her failing grades, so having them brought up by her mother definitely stung; (2) Anne reported that she characteristically shut down as soon as she sensed conflict, so when she perceived that she was under attack when her mother brought up her poor school performance, she felt overwhelmed ("I just couldn't take it"); (3) Anne then stated that because she knew she had been doing poorly in school and that her mom was, in theory, "right," she was unable to argue with her, leading her to think that she had nothing valid to say in response. In short, she felt helpless and incapable of expressing herself. So, in probing the information that Anne had already given us about her self-injury, we were able to arrive not only at the antecedent event but also at the emotions and thoughts that likely contributed to her cutting.

Next, we had Anne list specifically what she was feeling and thinking right after the interaction with her mom. Initially, she said, "I felt awful! How would you feel?" We countered by saying, "Well, if that happened to me I would have felt overwhelmed, helpless, angry, and like I wanted to escape that situation quickly." By really taking her perspective, we were able to understand and validate her emotions, which allowed her to accept them more easily. This encouraged Anne to work on specifically identifying her feelings.

We then went through a similar process for identifying her thoughts, trying to get her to pinpoint specific cognitions or beliefs that she had during or about the situation. Anne caught on quickly and stated that she had thought, "My mom doesn't understand that I feel terrible about my grades and that riding my case about it only makes me feel worse." She continued, "I wanted to tell her I knew she was right, but that I am having a hard enough time just physically getting to and staying in school right now, so trying to get high marks is a little lower on my priority list." Also, Anne stated that during the confrontation, she repetitively thought, "Just leave me alone. I wish you would just see my pain and stop." However, because she assumed that her low grades would invalidate anything she had to say in her mom's eyes, she failed to express herself.

After clearly identifying the antecedent events and her thoughts and feelings surrounding these events, we then focused on her behavior—cutting—and asked Anne to tell us exactly what had happened next. She reported that after the discussion with her mother, she had walked into the bathroom, taken out a razor, and cut herself "until [she] felt calmer." Then she poured peroxide on her injuries, covered them with bandages, and went right back into the kitchen, where her mother was sitting. Now that we had the facts, we focused on the immediate consequence of her cutting, or the feeling of increased calmness.

At this point, we tried to get her to identify what she had hoped to accomplish by cutting. After having broken the episode down this far, Anne was able to state that she had wanted her mother to stop berating her about her grades and thought that she would do so when she saw her injuries. She had thought that her mother would get the message that the whole conversation was too much for Anne and that she had obviously exceeded her emotional limit. Also, Anne had thought that her mother might try to take care of her when she saw Anne's injuries. Finally, Anne had also wanted her mother to feel guilty for having brought up such an uncomfortable topic in such a confrontational way.

Next, we focused on the other consequences of her self-injury—whether or not she had achieved her goals. Basically, Anne's mother had "flipped out" when she learned that Anne had cut herself, which only contributed to Anne's feeling lousy. So getting her mother to back off by cutting had failed abysmally. In addition, instead of taking pity on her and trying to nurture her, Anne's mom had become even more irritated and angry. Mission not accomplished. Anne had then reacted by screaming at her mother that she hated her, herself, and her life. At the point that Anne said these things, they were quite likely true. In fact, we would agree that she was probably feeling both helpless and hopeless. However, telling her mom that she hated her, her own life, and herself did not get Anne the sympathy or nurturing that she wanted either.

Anne said that she thought that she had met the goal of making her mother feel guilty, because her mother had begun crying. However, we were quick to bring up some alternative hypotheses about why Anne's mother might have been crying, including feelings of frustration, helplessness, or simply anger. So Anne might not have met this goal either, and, even if she had, it cost her a lot emotionally.

We also tried to have Anne identify what her mother might have been trying to achieve (apart from making her feel "like crap," as Anne suggested) by starting a discussion about Anne's grades in the first place. We had Anne try to imagine why her mother would even care about her grades at all. Anne was able to arrive at the conclusion that her mother might be concerned because her grades used to mean a lot to Anne, because she knew that doing poorly in school was likely contributing to the pressure and distress that Anne was feeling, and because her mother simply wanted Anne to be able to go to the college of her choice, which was not a possibility with failing grades.

Anne realized that she did not object that much to what her mom was probably trying to say but she recognized that she was feeling hurt because she felt attacked when her mom started stating that Anne was failing academically. Anne admitted that this had hit a nerve, and as a result her brain had taken this statement and run with it, so that she interpreted it to mean that she was a failure. We agreed that Anne's mom did not go about addressing these concerns in the best way, since her care and concern for Anne's well-being never came through. (She herself stated that she had not meant to sound so critical and disapproving but was having a hard time expressing herself to her estranged daughter. We actually spent time working with her to help her express her own thoughts and feelings more effectively.)

Finally, we tried to help Anne identify what she might do differently the next time this issue (or a similar one) came up. For example, we asked her how she might have articulated her thoughts and feelings to her mother. She stated that this would be very hard for her, since she tends to lock up during confrontations. We then addressed Anne's difficulties with expressing herself during confrontations by working on some methods of direct and assertive communication. We also worked with her to map out a dialogue with her mother to help her achieve the goals that she had hoped to accomplish by cutting (although we did question her goal of "making" her mother feel guilt or anything else, for that matter, since other people's feelings are their responsibility and are generally not under our control). We also stressed that if she were able to communicate more effectively, she would. We talked about some strategies for use when effective communication with the other party isn't working. We made suggestions for ways that she could extract herself from a situation *before* she hit her absolute limit. In addition, we worked with her to help her identify some activities that might ease her through difficult emotions that result from her limits being pushed.

Dialectical behavior therapy (Linehan 1993a, 1993b) may be palatable to even the most emotionally dysregulated adolescents (our toughest customers), because the therapist is not very "therapisty" but is instead very real and accessible. The feedback that we have received from our patients who have participated in DBT programs, particularly from teens who have a lot of interpersonal issues (including, but not limited to, borderline personality disorder), has told us that this approach works because the therapist acts as more of a teacher and a coach. As a result, the patient doesn't feel judged and is more likely to take the advice and practice the techniques. If you are considering DBT as a treatment option for your child, we highly recommend that you find professionals who can both do individual DBT and direct you to an adolescent DBT group, since DBT works best when done in a combination of individual and group settings.

For additional support in finding treatment professionals who practice CBT and DBT, contact the Association for Behavioral and Cognitive Therapies at www.aabt.org (go to the "Find a Therapist" link to find someone with the qualifications you need in your state). We

also find that the Obsessive-Compulsive Foundation (www
.ocfoundation.org) is an excellent resource. Though your child may not
have OCD, individuals trained to treat this disorder are generally
trained in CBT and have experience with self-injury. For DBT specialists and resources, we suggest consulting www.bpdcentral.com, a Web
site designed for individuals with borderline personality disorder, which
can be very helpful when you're trying to locate more information
about self-injury and treatment options.

IS HOSPITALIZATION NECESSARY?

What a frightening question. You probably never thought you'd ever
be considering this issue when you took on the adventure of parent-
hood. However, if your child is engaging in self-injury, you may indeed
have to ask and ultimately answer this question at some point in the
near future. As parents ourselves, we can only imagine how incredibly
painful it must be to have to evaluate your own child for suicidality
and hospitalization.

If and when you find yourself in this position, there are some key
points to remember that will help you hold it together as you take care
of your child.

- **Don't play the blame game!** Trying to figure out who is
  at fault for your child's self-injury will keep you from
  tuning in to your child sufficiently. You need to be fully
  present so you can make the necessary life-altering or
  life-saving decisions for your child.

- **Don't ask for (or accept) too many opinions.** Because
  time and your mental clarity are of the essence, don't stop
  to get opinions from everyone you know. Trust your judgment, follow the steps in this book, and consult a professional if necessary.

- **Try not to get stuck on making the perfect decision.**
  You are probably in one of the toughest situations of your
  life. If you allow your decisions to be governed by a combination of logic and love, they will be fine (not always
  perfect, but definitely adequate).

When you get to the point where you're considering hospitalization as an option for your child, it's safe to assume things have gotten pretty unstable and very scary. Generally, hospitalization becomes a potential short-term solution in the following situations:

- Your child is unable to commit to or succeed at keeping himself safe, despite having made commitments to do so.

- Your child is self-injuring to the point of causing serious physical harm that requires medical attention.

- Your child is unable to stop hurting himself for more than a day.

- Your child is engaging in other behaviors that pose an imminent risk to his health (such as starvation, drug or alcohol abuse, or allowing himself to be abused by others).

- Your child's reality testing or impulse control is impaired (for example, your child is manic; your child's judgment is affected by substance use; or your child is out of touch with reality due to dissociation, psychosis, or the effects of drugs or alcohol).

- Your child is saying that he wants to kill himself. This is different than saying that he wants to die, because *wanting to die* is passive, while actually thinking about killing oneself is active and may imply the intention to do so.

Notice that we stated that hospitalization is a *potential short-term solution*. It is something to consider when your child's self-injury is at a point where he is no longer in control, and you don't feel capable of keeping him safe. Keep in mind that hospitalization may be just the beginning of treatment. No child we've ever known has emerged from the hospital 100 percent "cured," in control, and not in need of further psychological treatment. In fact, the hospital stay is really only helpful with providing immediate protection for your child, possibly getting him on a medication regimen, and caring for his most basic needs (nutrition, sleep, detoxing from drugs and/or alcohol, and safety) until he is able to come home to pursue outpatient treatment.

Your child may resent your decision to go with hospitalization, especially if his dangerous behavior may be his only way of coping with painful emotions and difficult events. Please don't let this resistance discourage you from pursuing this avenue of care. As you know, there are lots of things that benefit your child's health that he may not like, or that may upset him significantly; however, this does not mean that you should avoid doing them. If you relented just because they protested, your children would probably not be vaccinated, see the dentist, eat broccoli, or go to bed at a reasonable hour. And, as you also know, children and adolescents, especially those in crisis, don't usually make the best decisions for themselves. Case in point: your child has chosen to cut or otherwise hurt himself as a coping strategy.

Adolescents in crisis can be very vehement in their protests against getting the treatment they really need, and the strength of their arguments can test even the most stalwart parent. One of us once had to spend about an hour on the phone with a suicidal patient (a very bright, articulate fifteen-year-old engaging in self-injury up to five times a day), challenging her assertion that self-injury was actually *beneficial* as a coping strategy to keep her from killing herself. After first stating her position calmly, then bargaining, begging, threatening to disown her mother and never come to therapy again, and cursing out both her mother and her therapist for trying to control her and "institutionalize [her] like a mental patient," she finally went to the hospital. After about two weeks on an adolescent inpatient unit, she was discharged and then was placed in a residential therapeutic school, which she attended for nine months before going back to her district high school. She participated in intensive DBT outpatient therapy for one year, with another year of weekly sessions. She is currently maintaining her gains in weekly individual therapy sessions. Now, she is achieving high marks in college, has been abstinent from self-injury for approximately five years, and (believe it or not) is still in contact with her psychologist and has not disowned her mother to date.

One last word on hospitalization: know your area hospitals. If you are even thinking of hospitalization as an outside possibility, it's better to be prepared by learning what resources are available to you. Find out what hospitals are in your area and whether they have adolescent psychiatric units. Also, if you are working with a professional, find out if that person is affiliated with any area hospitals, and which he or she recommends for your child's specific issues. Finally, make a list of support resources. These might include the following phone numbers and other information:

- The phone number of the emergency room of a hospital with an adolescent inpatient unit near you. If you have the opportunity to call ahead it can save you some time once you get there.

- The phone number of the mobile crisis unit in your city or county. This is a group of individuals trained to intervene during crisis situations, who will come to your home if you are concerned about taking your child to the hospital yourself but don't think the risk is imminent enough to call 911.

- The number of a close friend or family member. Choose someone who is aware of the situation and who can come at a moment's notice to take care of your other children or commitments, or who might accompany you on the ride to the hospital.

- The number for your local police and ambulance if your community does not have 911 service. Keep this number handy if the situation is a dangerous one, or if you are concerned that your child might behave dangerously or might escalate the dangerous behavior when you propose hospitalization.

- Driving directions to the hospital, so that if you need to exercise that option you won't have to worry about getting directions or reading maps.

HOW TO ASSESS FOR SUICIDALITY

You probably can't believe you may ever have to do this. Hopefully, you won't. However, if you do not have a treatment professional available and you fear that your child is at immediate risk of inflicting serious and potentially fatal injury to himself, you may need to assess his current level of suicidality in order to choose a course of action. The first question to ask your child is if he has been thinking about suicide. If the answer is yes, the acronym SLAP (Miller 1985) will serve as a quick reminder of questions you'll need to ask in order to do a basic suicide assessment.

- **S—Specificity of suicide plan.** Ask your child if he has been thinking seriously about suicide or about dying more than previously. If he states he has been thinking about actively taking his life, continue questioning him. You might say, "You said that you've been thinking about suicide. Do you mean actually killing yourself, or just wishing that you were dead?" Try to find out if your child has a specific plan and means in mind (in other words, when, where, and how he plans to attempt suicide).

- **L—Lethality of means.** Some plans are clearly more lethal than others. For example, slitting his wrists, shooting himself, jumping in front of a train, or hanging himself would be more worrisome than a less articulated method, such as "I don't know; I'll hold my breath until I run out of air." This is probably one of the harder questions you'll ever ask, but you might want to phrase it something like this: "I know you said you want to kill yourself. I hate to even ask this, but I really want to know how you would do it. What is your plan?" Take all suicidal ideation seriously, but act quickly if your child has a clear and dangerous means in mind.

- **A—Availability of the means.** Ask your child if he has access to the intended means for his suicide. If you have a gun in the house, and he has stated that he has chosen to use that weapon to kill himself, waste no time in getting him to a hospital and getting the gun out of the house.

- **P—Proximity of help.** Evaluate the availability of helping resources. For example, if it's three in the morning, your child's therapist (who is usually available during crisis situations) is on vacation, and your child refuses to speak to the on-call psychologist, you might make a different decision than you would if the regular therapist were only a phone call away.

Make a copy of the SLAP suicide assessment plan above. Though it may sound corny, use it to guide your questions if you think that your child may be suicidal. Better to look corny than to miss asking an important question that could save your child's life.

SUICIDE ASSESSMENT
(SLAP)

Specificity of suicide plan.

Lethality of means.

Availability of the means.

Proximity of help.

If, after doing the SLAP assessment, you decide that your child is in danger of attempting suicide, be prepared to take him to the hospital.

Make sure you're not alone when you make the trip to the hospital with your child. This is important for two reasons. First, it's good to have someone there to support both you and your child in this difficult decision. Sometimes, we get so wrapped up in our own self-doubt or pain or guilt that we need someone to remind us that we really are good parents and that we really are doing the right thing. It's also helpful for the child to have someone to support, talk to, and attend to him while you are focused on getting him to the hospital safely. Second, in addition to providing moral support, an extra body can provide necessary physical support: the closer you get to the hospital, the more real the decision becomes, and it is at this point that some individuals may try to escape. Having a strong, supportive person sitting with your child allows you to focus on driving and not worry about your child trying to jump out of the car or run away in the parking lot.

If you are not feeling strong enough to drive, or if you think that your child might need your full attention, call a car service such as a taxi, ask a family member or friend to drive you to the hospital, or call an ambulance. We always encourage parents to err on the side of caution and safety.

If your child refuses to go to the hospital, if you do not think he is capable of keeping himself safe because his judgment is compromised (due to intoxication or psychosis), or if he is actively engaged in a suicidal gesture or attempt (such as threatening himself with a knife or overdosing on medication), call 911 for an ambulance and the police immediately. Many parents resist this option, though it is probably the best choice in an emergency situation, because they are concerned about what the neighbors will think seeing their child being escorted into an ambulance or a police car. Though we know that this can be embarrassing, we ask you to consider your child's safety first and think about how you will deal with the neighbors later (or *if* you will deal with the neighbors, since it's really none of their business).

If you do the SLAP assessment and you get the sense that your child is being totally honest with you and is not in imminent danger of attempting suicide, breathe a sigh of relief. It's likely that hospitalization is not currently a necessity. However, maintaining an open discussion about suicide is still advisable. This doesn't necessarily mean that every morning before school you say, "Good morning, sweetheart. Would you like cereal or eggs, and, by the way, are you planning to kill yourself today?" That would just be unhealthy and your child would quickly regret ever sharing that thought with you. However, you will want to inquire about his level of suicidality at times when you notice your child in emotional distress, or in a state of increased agitation.

We know you would rather not talk to your child about taking his own life. It will be disturbing and painful for both you and him. We've worked with a lot of parents who were afraid to ask their kids about suicide because they feared that by speaking about it they might stimulate suicidal thinking in their children. We understand this fear. However, there is no evidence to support that talking about suicide causes it. In fact, if your children know that they can approach you about this issue, it could save their lives.

WHEN HOSPITALIZATION IS UNNECESSARY

There are situations when hospitalization is not the best option. Generally, it is safe to assume that hospitalization would be ill advised and would probably be considered therapeutic overkill when your child:

- Actively engages in treatment with a professional who is closely managing the case

- Commits to and follows through with keeping himself safe

8

What to Expect During Treatment

Congratulations! You've arrived at the point where you can start treatment for your child. But where to start, and what will treatment entail?

Our best advice is to make an appointment for a psychological evaluation. When a psychologist meets with you and your child, he or she will be assessing your child's thoughts, emotional experiences, and behaviors in order to make the appropriate diagnosis, decide the best course of treatment, and determine whether a referral to a psychiatrist is necessary.

Comprehensive treatment for self-injury and its related disorders includes effective psychologically based treatments and sometimes medication. We say "sometimes" because in some cases CBT or DBT may be enough to address your child's needs. However, as we've alluded to throughout the book, some people who self-injure have psychiatric conditions that require medication management. Without medication, these people are unable to benefit from therapy or even function adequately on a daily basis. If your child's qualified psychologist determines that medication is a necessary part of your child's treatment, her psychologist will refer her to a psychiatrist or psychopharmacologist to further evaluate her and decide on an appropriate medication regimen.

Psychologists are trained in assessment, diagnosis, and treatment of psychological disorders and will do the following:

1. Identify the specific symptoms your child is having (such as depression, problems with eating, anxiety, or other problems).

2. Evaluate your child for her level of health risk behaviors in addition to cutting (such as drug and alcohol use, risky sexual behaviors, or other parasuicidal behaviors).

3. Do a comprehensive suicide risk evaluation.

4. Evaluate the need for hospitalization.

5. Evaluate the need for a medication consultation and make a referral if necessary.

6. Develop a plan for comprehensive treatment of your child's self-injury and related psychological diagnoses.

A psychiatrist or psychopharmacologist is a medical doctor who is trained to do the following:

1. Conduct a psychiatric evaluation.

2. Provide a diagnosis.

3. Determine whether or not medication is necessary and what medication choices are most prudent.

4. Prescribe medication.

5. Monitor medication administration and side effects.

Now that you know what psychologists and psychiatrists do, you'll be better prepared to make informed choices about your child's care—when you're first choosing, and later working with, a mental health professional.

THE INITIAL CONSULTATION

Let's talk about the initial consultation. Before the appointment, there are some things that you and your child can do to prepare yourselves, so you can gain the maximum benefit from your time spent in that appointment. Here is a list of questions that will help you and your child prepare for the initial consultation.

- What type of emotional distress is your child experiencing on a daily basis?

  - Does she feel depressed or sad?

  - Is she nervous or anxious?

  - Is she experiencing any obsessive thinking (repetitive anxiety-provoking thoughts that she just can't get out of her head)?

  - Is she engaging in any compulsive behaviors (repetitive anxiety-neutralizing acts)?

  - Is she feeling intensely and inexplicably angry or numb?

  - Is she feeling like she wants to harm herself? (You might have already covered this in your suicide assessment. If not, now is a good time to do so.)

- How long has she been feeling this way (for example, a few weeks, several months, or a year)?

- Was there a trigger or event that led her to feel this way?

- How are her thoughts, feelings, or behaviors interfering with her daily functioning?

  - Are her difficulties affecting her academically?

  - Is she becoming socially isolated or has she lost friends?

  - Is she fighting with family and/or friends?

  - Has she lost enjoyment in activities that she previously thought were fun or stopped a hobby or significant interest?

- Is she avoiding people, places, or situations?

- Are her difficulties affecting her sleeping or appetite?

■ Get the specifics about her self-injury.

- What types of self-injury has she engaged in?

- How does she self-injure?

- How often does she self-injure?

- When does she self-injure?

- Why does she self-injure? (In other words, what are her triggers?)

- How many times has she self-injured?

■ Is she engaging in any other health risk behaviors?

- Is she drinking?

- Is she using drugs?

- Is she driving while intoxicated, or driving recklessly?

- Is she engaging in risky sexual behaviors?

- Is she eating properly?

- Is she sleeping enough?

■ Is she happy with her body in general, her appearance, and her weight?

■ Is she in danger of being hurt by anyone else? (Has anyone ever threatened to hurt her, or actually hurt her? Does she feel threatened by anyone in any way?)

Ideally, of course, your child will sit down with you before the initial consultation to go through this checklist with you. However, we'd venture to guess that she may be unwilling to do this. If this is the case, please don't push it. You might want to have her look it over so she is prepared for some of the questions that she will be asked but, if she is absolutely against it, it's no great tragedy. Most people don't come to their initial consultation appointment this prepared. We are simply suggesting this type of preparation so that you and your child will know what to expect and be able to provide the most accurate information.

Other things you might want to think about in advance are her medical history (and current medications, if relevant), her history of previous psychological issues, and any psychological illnesses in the family. This doesn't mean that every skeleton in your family's proverbial closet will have to be aired during the consultation. However, the more information you can provide to the psychologist regarding similar difficulties experienced by other members of your nuclear or extended family, the better. Specifically, think about whether anyone in your family suffered from anything similar during their adolescence. Also, we urge you to make the consulting clinician aware if there is any family history of suicide. We don't mean to scare you, but we do need to let you know that a family history of suicide can be a risk factor for your immediate family members.

If your child has a history of physical, emotional, or sexual abuse, and you think that she might be too embarrassed to report it during the consultation, be prepared to disclose this information to the psychologist as well. You may choose to do this during the phone intake (when you schedule the consult), or you may ask to have a word alone with the provider toward the end of the consultation, but don't let the appointment end without letting the psychologist know.

Recognize that you are meeting with a trained professional, and that you are probably in good hands. We find that some parents are so anxious and eager to make sure that their children are getting the right help that they try to set the agenda for the initial appointment. Though we totally understand the emotional reasons behind this, it's generally better if you allow the clinician to ask the questions. Be forewarned that the clinician may ask for some time alone with your child. This can be helpful, because your child might disclose more if she views the psychologist, not you, as the one in control (especially if she is resentful of or angry with you, or if she feels like she is disappointing you or letting you down). This can also be beneficial if your child feels uncomfortable speaking in front of you. Getting an opportunity to have the psychologist's ear to herself may allow your child to let down her guard enough to disclose some important information. Don't worry— the psychologist is ethically bound to inform you if your child is in any danger or risk of danger, so you won't be kept in the dark if there is something you really need to know. Generally, we provide both the child and her parents with the opportunity to have some private time with the clinician, as well as some time together to discuss all issues, during the first appointment.

Consultation appointments usually last about an hour and may take as long as ninety minutes, depending on the amount of information that needs to be covered. After the consultation, you can expect to receive your child's diagnosis, a plan for her future therapy sessions, and referrals to any relevant treatment services (such as group therapy, drug and alcohol counseling, a program for treating eating disorders, a psychiatric consult, a physician consult, or referral for inpatient or intensive therapy). If she is going to be receiving therapy with the consulting psychologist or at his or her facility, the frequency (one or more individual therapy sessions per week) and duration of treatment will also be discussed.

PSYCHIATRIC CONSULTATION

If your child's psychologist refers her for psychiatric consultation, this does not mean that she is beyond psychological help or that she is suicidal. It may simply mean the psychologist recognizes that (1) she may not achieve the maximum desired benefit from therapy alone, (2) she might respond better to therapy if certain symptoms were being addressed by medication, or (3) her symptoms are severe enough to warrant the use of both medication and CBT or DBT. Whatever the case, if a medication consultation is recommended, don't panic.

We know that it's a very big deal to consider having your child take psychotropic medication (medications that can alter psychological functioning), especially an antidepressant, with all of the recent negative media attention regarding increased risk of suicide in certain teens. However, if your child is scrupulously monitored by the treating physician, you administer the medication consistently, and you immediately report all side effects or rapid changes in your child's personality and behavior to the treating clinician, this will be less of an issue.

Of course, you're still reluctant to put your child on medication. We understand. However, think of it this way: Imagine that your child had cancer and you found out that the chemotherapy, which could save her life, could also make her sick and weaken her. Would you opt to skip it? Probably not. You would probably just pay very close attention to any and all reactions to the medication and keep in close contact with her doctors. That's the same approach we recommend for individuals whose children are on psychotropic medications.

Also, you'd never allow your child's chemotherapy for cancer to be prescribed or monitored by her pediatrician or by your family practitioner, right? Of course not—you'd seek the expertise of an experienced and well-trained pediatric oncologist. Similarly, we strongly recommend that you use a psychiatrist or psychopharmacologist to prescribe psychotropic medications to your child. We know this means yet another doctor visit (and bill), but the proper administration and monitoring of this class of medications is absolutely critical for your child's health.

Your child's comfort with the psychiatrist is also important. Hopefully, you will have found a pediatric psychiatrist or psychopharmacologist (perhaps through your insurance company's referral service) who is accustomed to speaking with and working with children or adolescents. If your child is old enough to see her prescribing physician alone and is uncomfortable with this, ask her if your presence during her appointments would help. Otherwise, find someone both you and your child can be comfortable and open with. While choosing a prescribing physician is not as crucial as selecting a therapist (because you will see the psychiatrist or psychopharmacologist far less often, only about once or twice a month), it is critical that your and your child's rapport with that person is positive, because of the importance of reporting side effects and medication efficacy.

What types of medications might be prescribed to my child?

There are no medications specifically designed to stop cutting, since cutting is generally a behavioral expression of other types of underlying psychological distress. Therefore, the medications that we see most frequently being prescribed to self-injuring individuals tend to fall into three categories, based on the symptoms they are designed to address, discussed below.

ANTIDEPRESSANTS

Antidepressant medications, as the name suggests, are designed to treat depressive symptoms. However, because depression and anxiety are biologically linked by the brain chemical serotonin (see chapter 2), antidepressant medications are also prescribed to treat anxiety disorders like obsessive-compulsive disorder, panic disorder, posttraumatic stress disorder, social phobia, and generalized anxiety disorder. The antidepressants include the medications referred to as selective serotonin reuptake inhibitors, or SSRIs (such as Prozac, Paxil, Luvox, Zoloft, Celexa, and Lexapro), but they also include older medications like the tricyclic antidepressants (such as nortriptyline and Anafranil), as well as those that affect other neurochemicals, like norepinephrine (such as Effexor and Wellbutrin). Some new combination medications (like Cymbalta) that have recently come on to the market combine SSRIs with low-dose antipsychotic medications; however, they are not yet being used on children and adolescents, so we will not address them here.

Psychopharmacologists and psychiatrists are most likely to prescribe the SSRIs to children and adolescents suffering from either depression or anxiety disorders, since they tend to have lower side-effect profiles than the older tricyclic antidepressants, in addition to their being effective at reducing depressive symptoms, anxiety, and obsessive thinking and compulsive behaviors. Currently, the only SSRI approved for the treatment of depression in children and adolescents is Prozac, which has been around for almost fifteen years and is the oldest of the SSRIs. Luvox, which is currently only available in its generic form, fluvoxamine, was the first medication approved for the treatment of OCD in children and is also often used to treat depression. In addition, Zoloft is frequently prescribed to children with anxiety and depressive symptoms. As we mentioned in chapter 2, Paxil is currently contraindicated in children and adolescents, because of several cases involving children who became aggressive and suicidal while taking this medication.

As a class of medications, the SSRIs can be very effective in treating anxiety and depression. However, children with a biological predisposition to bipolar disorder (formerly referred to as "manic depression") may develop mania while on these medications. In addition, isolated cases of children attempting and completing suicide on SSRIs have led to increased caution when clinicians are prescribing this class of medication. If you have a family history of suicide or bipolar disorder, make your prescribing psychiatrist or psychopharmacologist aware of this fact during your child's initial medication consult. Otherwise, close monitoring of your child's behavior and medication use by your physician can help to minimize the risks associated with these medications.

Medications like Effexor and Wellbutrin are less often prescribed to young children but may be prescribed to teenagers. They work similarly to, but are chemically different from, the SSRIs, so some physicians prescribe them for those who have trouble tolerating the SSRIs. They may also be used in small doses to boost the effects of SSRIs.

The tricyclic antidepressants like Anafranil and nortriptyline are not usually prescribed for children. However, we have found that many children who become hyperactive, agitated, and even aggressive while taking SSRIs may tolerate Anafranil better, because it is less serotonin binding. Anafranil was the first medication in history approved to treat OCD, and it is still considered an effective pharmacological intervention for this disorder, but it comes with increased likelihood of side effects like dry mouth, constipation, and weight gain. We hardly ever see nortriptyline being prescribed to children or teens, which is a good thing, because it is associated with much more frequent and severe side effects than the other medications we've discussed.

Regardless of what antidepressant medication your child has been prescribed, there are some important things to remember:

- All of these medications are most effective when they are allowed to build up in the system and therefore have to be taken consistently (every day, at the same time of day) and as they are prescribed in order to work properly.

- As a result, it may take more than six weeks for your child to begin to feel any difference in her mood or anxiety level, so don't give up if it doesn't seem like it's working right away.

- The rule of thumb for these medications, especially with children and adolescents, is to start low, and go slow. If it seems like your psychiatrist or psychopharmacologist is dragging his or her heels about increasing your child's dose, the professional is probably doing a good job.

- Less is more. When a child seems to be getting some relief at a lower dose of medication, this does not mean that she will get even better results at a higher dose (especially if that amount exceeds the dosing guidelines).

■ The most common side effects of these medications, such as headache, nausea, diarrhea, and sleepiness or sleep disturbance, go away within about two weeks and may reoccur if your child stops taking her medication abruptly.

■ The side effects you should be concerned about include rapid personality changes, agitation, irritability, intense and unexplained anger, suicidality, aggression toward others, sleeplessness, and mania. If these occur, report them to your psychiatrist or psychopharmacologist immediately.

■ Alcohol, illicit drugs, and other medications can alter the effectiveness of antidepressants and may be dangerous in combination with them. If you suspect that your child is using other substances, or if your child has been prescribed other medications, always let the treating physician know.

■ Make sure that your child takes all medications as prescribed. Stopping or decreasing some of these medications abruptly may pose a danger to your child's health. Do not allow her to decrease or discontinue use of any medication without the supervision of the prescribing physician.

ANXIOLYTICS

This class of medication is also referred to as the antianxiety drugs. These are generally mild sedatives that belong to the class called the benzodiazepines and include medications like Valium, Xanax, Klonopin, Ativan, and Ambien. They work very differently than the antidepressants in that they are effective about thirty minutes after being taken, and they often wear off in a few (generally six to eight) hours. By blocking the body's excitatory nervous system response, they reduce the physiological and psychological experience of anxiety. They may also be used to assist people in falling asleep.

Of these, Klonopin is most often prescribed to children, even very young children, though Xanax is also used in children and adolescents. Benzodiazepines in general are effective and fast acting, so they tend to be prescribed to those who are experiencing panic attacks and intense, situational anxiety. However, all of the benzodiazepines are habit forming if taken consistently for more than ten days, and they carry with them the risk of seizure if they are rapidly withdrawn after this time period. Because of their addictive potential, they are meant for short-term use and can be taken as needed, right before anxiety-provoking situations, or to induce sleep.

They can be lethal if mixed with alcohol, or if they are taken in very high doses. Therefore, if you suspect that your child is using alcohol, tell her about this risk and address your concerns with her psychiatrist or psychopharmacologist.

Some teens abuse the benzodiazepines in order to get high. If your child has been prescribed one of these medications and she must take it at some point during the day when you cannot supervise her (for example, at school), then have another responsible adult keep and administer the medication (the school nurse, for example). If you are concerned that your child might be abusing her prescription, you may also want to keep a running tally of the remaining number of pills each day in a private location, or keep the medication in a place that only you know about, so you can control its dispensation.

MOOD STABILIZERS

The mood stabilizers, which are not really one class of medication, help to level out severe mood swings, reduce manic symptoms, and decrease the impulsivity, irritability, and agitation often associated with mood disorders, borderline personality disorder, and impulse control disorders. One of the most well-known mood stabilizers is Lithium, which is actually a naturally occurring compound. This medication is used to treat bipolar disorder but may be used in small doses with antidepressants. Lithium, however, is not very widely prescribed in children and adolescents, because of its side-effect profile (which can include weight gain and acne).

Other mood stabilization agents include the anticonvulsants, or medications that are used to control seizures. In lower doses these medications can be very effective at stabilizing mood (bringing down the highs associated with mania, as well as reducing impulsivity, irritability, and aggression). The anticonvulsants that tend to be used as mood stabilizers in children and adolescents include, but are not limited to, Topamax, Trileptal, Tenex, Depakote, and Lamictal.

Sometimes these medications are given to children who have manic-type reactions to the SSRIs, in order to allow them to continue on those medications, by controlling their adverse side effects. Other times these are given alone to address the mood instability that may be present in individuals who self-injure and have major mood swings, poor impulse control, and explosive behavior.

Finally, some psychiatrists and psychopharmacologists are beginning to prescribe Abilify to their child and adolescent patients for mood stabilization. Unlike Lithium and the anticonvulsants, it is actually an atypical antipsychotic that has mood-stabilizing qualities in low doses. It can be given in conjunction with antidepressants and even other mood stabilizers to improve their efficacy.

Many of our adolescent self-injurers have reported reduced emotional intensity as well as decreased urges to cut while on mood stabilizers. However, individuals who are truly bipolar tend not to like these medications, because while taking these agents they feel blunted, like someone took the edge off their mania. As a result, they may not comply with their medication regimens. Also, combining alcohol or other drugs with mood stabilizers can make a person quite ill, so again we urge you to warn your child about these dangers if you're concerned about drug or alcohol use.

GENERAL GUIDELINES FOR MEDICATING YOUR CHILD

We strongly urge you to be involved in the administration of your child's medication. Know when and how she takes it, and how much she is taking. Close supervision of any medication regimen can ensure that it is effective.

Sometimes, however, getting your child to take the medication that has been prescribed for her can be a major battle. So many children and adolescents feel stigmatized enough by the fact that they are experiencing psychological difficulties and are participating in therapy that taking medication seems just too humiliating. In the face of such strong resistance, you may find that getting your child to take medication is a battle that you just don't want to fight. However, if you have been referred for a medication consult and that physician has deemed that your child is in need of medication, then it is very likely an important issue and a battle worth fighting.

Actually, we don't recommend fighting about it. Rather, we recommend that you reason with your child. Let her know that her particular issue is, like diabetes, biologically based, and that if she had diabetes—even if she hated finger sticks and taking insulin—you'd insist, because without these measures she could become more ill or die. This is a very difficult metaphor for a child to argue with. Let your child know that you understand how she feels, and that you wouldn't like to take medication either. Stress just how much you love her and tell her that giving a child necessary medication to help her get through a rough time is just what a good parent does.

Ultimately, you can't really force your child to take her medication. If refusing to take it puts her in danger (as it would in the case of an impulsive, suicidal child with bipolar disorder, for example), then you might need to consider hospitalization. Her prescribing physician should be notified if this is the case, so that he or she can become involved and take the appropriate action if necessary.

If your child doesn't like a certain side effect or feeling that she experiences on any given medication, encourage her to communicate with her psychiatrist or psychopharmacologist as well. The more open their rapport, the better able the physician will be to explain, in a way that makes sense to your child, why certain medications are effective and advisable.

Determining your role in therapy lies partly in trusting yourself as a parent, assessing the type of relationship you have with your child, and becoming comfortable with the new skills you have learned from this and other books. In general, therapists do believe that family involvement can have a great impact on a person's treatment progress. We have limited contact with our patients on a weekly basis, whereas the family has the luxury of seeing the patient under a variety of circumstances and for an extended duration. This proximity provides you with the ability to observe your child's progress and report back to the therapist as well as the opportunity to reinforce the skills your child is learning in therapy. Assessing our patients' treatment progress is more meaningful and accurate if people in their lives can corroborate what we observe during our therapeutic contact. So, should you stay out of your child's therapy completely and just sit in the waiting room week after week? The answer to that question is a resounding no.

You're probably wondering, "Sure, of course I want to be involved in my child's life and his treatment progress, but how do I do that and to what degree?" Well, the degree of involvement may differ during the different phases of treatment.

INITIAL STAGES OF THERAPY

The general goal in the initial stages of therapy is to gather relevant information, build rapport, and educate the patient about treatment. In this phase, your feedback to the therapist is a very important part of the treatment plan. It's not unreasonable to ask for some time during the initial visit to meet with the therapist to share your child's psychological, academic, medical, and social history as well as their current life situation. This is a standard practice in the first appointment for most mental health professionals. If you believe you need more time, or if you would like this to happen regularly, then you'll need to schedule your own time to speak to the therapist. In the early stages of treatment, we often make separate appointments for parents so that they can fill us in on how their child is doing, ask questions, and get advice (preferably scheduled during a time when the child is at school or home—not sitting in the waiting room or the therapy room).

In addition, in the early phase of therapy, spend some time with the therapist learning the types of activities your child will be doing during an actual therapy session. You'll find that having this information diminishes the urge you may have to grill your child about what transpired behind the therapist's closed door, and it also gives you some base of knowledge to draw from when your child chooses to disclose various details of his session. You'll want to become familiar with the therapy "language," since this will be an integral part of your child's life as well. In order for you to provide consistency between therapy and home by reinforcing the use of therapeutic skills to address the self-injury, it is helpful to know what therapy is *really* about, and conversations with your child's therapist are a good first step.

These initial stages of treatment also provide the perfect opportunity for you to clarify many of your questions regarding your role in treatment. Discuss it during joint therapy appointments with your child. Ask what helps him, what bothers him, and what he would prefer that you do or refrain from week after week. Setting the appropriate boundaries now will help everyone feel more in control of the therapy process. Find out whether your child will be comfortable having discussions with you about the content of his sessions. Ask him what level of detail he is willing to share with you. It can't hurt your relationship with your child to admit that you do have questions and doubts about how to handle the very difficult issues you're both facing. Ask for concrete and specific answers to your questions. The therapist can guide your child and you to have a productive conversation to resolve these issues.

Many years of psychological research have demonstrated that the therapeutic relationship has a powerful impact on a person's treatment progress. Your child's progress does depend partly on his ability to trust his therapist, believe she or he is a competent, qualified professional, and to feel comfortable and safe in a therapeutic session. It is important that you foster this relationship during the initial phases of treatment. You can do this by sticking to the agreed-upon boundaries and by respecting his need to have a private and independent relationship with his therapist. He may turn to his therapist for help rather than giving in to urges to self-injure. At times, you may end up feeling like the third wheel. This doesn't really mean that you are. It simply means that your child is bonding with his therapist and that he is using that relationship effectively. Parents who become threatened by, or who feel jealous and attempt to control, the therapeutic relationship between child and psychologist lessen the therapist's ability to develop a therapeutic alliance with the child.

If your child does share something about a therapy session that makes you uncomfortable or doubt the therapist's approach, we suggest that you address it directly with the therapist, rather than with your child. You have every right to disagree with something the therapist may have said to your child, but sharing your doubts with your child can affect the degree of respect your child has for his therapy. It is more helpful to clarify your concerns directly with the therapist without your child's knowledge.

It is normal for a parent, especially of a withdrawn or noncommunicative child, to feel envious of that child's open relationship with his therapist. At times when you and your child are in conflict, your child may use the therapist's advice or words to dispute something you've said, or he may make comments like "I'm calling my doctor. At least *she* understands me and doesn't yell at me or get mad at me." Such a statement would rattle even the most composed parent; however, remember that only you can parent and love your child. His therapist's job is to remain neutral and supportive, and to provide therapy, not parenting. Therefore, when you are angry about something your child has done, and his therapist remains calm when your child calls him, know that you are both doing your jobs well. You are perfectly within your rights to feel anger toward your child when he does something that provokes it, and you are also fulfilling your parental role when you provide him with negative consequences for behavior that is clearly not acceptable. As therapists, our job is not to parent but to examine behavior, break it down, restructure negative thinking, redirect maladaptive behaviors, and deescalate dangerous situations. Sometimes kids like the therapist's objective style rather than dealing on a more emotional level with their parents. That does not mean that they like us better than they like you.

SKILL-ACQUISITION AND SKILL-BUILDING PHASES OF THERAPY

As therapy progresses, your child will be learning and, hopefully, implementing some of the specific skills and strategies he needs in order to regulate his emotions and cope with urges to self-injure. You may certainly have additional questions as therapy becomes more focused on the specific symptoms and illness. You may have specific questions about how you can help at the very moment your child is struggling with an urge to cut or is having an emotionally difficult time. At this point in therapy, your involvement is not only helpful but crucial to his progress. Your observations of your child's behavior, changes in his emotional state, use of the strategies, and any changes in his life circumstances or stressful life events are important pieces of information to share with the therapist. You may have also observed some changes in the cutting itself that the therapist should know about, especially if it has become more frequent or intense and could be placing your child at an increased risk for suicide or death. In addition, you or your child may want to alter some of the boundaries set earlier in treatment. You may want to become more involved, your child may want you less involved, or the therapist may request more or less of your involvement as therapy progresses. The therapist may want your child to implement the strategies more independently, in which case less involvement would be called for. If your child, on the other hand, answers any of your questions by saying, "I'm not talking to you about this. Speak to my therapist," then more involvement may be necessary for you to become an integral part of the treatment.

Whether you meet alone with the therapist or with both the therapist and your child to address these ongoing issues is a function of the therapist's style, your child's preference, and yours. If there are topics that you are more comfortable discussing out of your child's presence, then request that some time be set aside for you at the end of the session. Similarly, the therapist may request to speak to you alone to discuss certain issues that would be better addressed in your child's absence. There are just certain things that kids don't need to be privy to, like household finances, parental conflict, and even a parent's venting about his or her own frustrations and limitations.

If you plan on asking for some private time with your child's therapist during his session, have a dialogue with your child either before or during the appointment to introduce this idea. Explain that you want to learn more about the therapy so that you can help support him throughout the process. Tell your child that you would like some guidance regarding changes that you may make in your own behavior in order to help him. (A side benefit of this approach is that it may help him to feel less targeted as the problem when he realizes that situations and people *other* than him may have to also change so he can get better.) If your child refuses, then inform the therapist about your desire to be involved and request that he or she address it with your child. You may have to be patient until the therapist believes that it is the proper time in treatment to involve you.

Most of the adolescents we have treated do accept their parents' involvement once they understand the therapeutic process and trust their therapist to maintain confidentiality. Most also desire that their parents acquire some of the skills they've learned in treatment so that the parent can help them implement the strategies they have been developing. Adolescents' overall need for their parents to understand them and support them, whether in therapy or in their everyday life, is a good reason for you to work to stay involved in your child's therapy. Discussing important issues and skills with the therapist, with your child's permission, will go a long way toward helping your child feel validated, supported, and understood.

RELAPSE PREVENTION

Once your child has been able to significantly reduce or prevent harmful and maladaptive behaviors, has acquired and is able to implement the necessary therapeutic skills, and has met the majority of his treatment goals, his therapist will probably introduce the concept of relapse prevention. The focus of relapse prevention is to help your child maintain his gains with a greater level of independence in both the short term and the long term.

In this stage, your child's therapist will teach him some new skills and strengthen the skills he has already acquired, including how to recognize the signs of a relapse, how to tell the difference between a setback and a relapse, and when to seek therapeutic help in the future. At this point, and with your and your child's consent, the therapist may start to decrease the frequency of sessions. Generally, this is only done once your child is showing competent and consistent practice of the relapse prevention skills, and once your child has been abstinent from self-injury for a specified amount of time. We usually suggest that our patients, especially children and adolescents, be free from self-injury for close to a year before we will consider them ready for a relapse prevention protocol.

Many of our patients maintain regular contact with us long after they have terminated active treatment. We encourage this ongoing contact, since it helps them to stay on top of their issues and to identify potential problems before they get hit by them with full force. They may come in for a session every four to six weeks, especially during stressful life periods such as starting college, getting married, or moving. Continued contact greatly increases the chances that your child can be free of self-injury, and it gives him an opportunity to revise and strengthen the skills he has already learned and apply them to new life situations.

As an involved parent, you'll find that all of these therapeutic skills your child is learning (which, we hope, you are learning yourself) will be helpful to you as well, for example, in helping you deal with your emotional reactions to the cutting, coping with frustration and hopelessness, and staying calm when your child doesn't seem to be making progress. Learning how to recognize the signs of a relapse are equally important for you to learn, since family members frequently recognize the signs before the person suffering from the illness does. There may be times when you want to know how to get your child back into treatment, if needed, especially since getting the process started the first time was probably very challenging. Staying involved as much as possible within the agreed-upon boundaries will allow you to help your child to the best of your ability.

SPECIFIC CONCERNS

You may have specific questions that go beyond the above guidelines. Below are answers to the most common questions asked by the parents of our patients.

How do I continue to validate?

As you may have already guessed, validation is a key factor in the therapeutic process. It is the one skill we spend a lot of time coaching our parents to implement. We incorporate it into every therapy session, so we encourage parents to also use it on a daily basis. This ensures continuity between the therapy sessions and the home environment, which is the only other place your child is likely to turn for support and understanding. Using validation at home will give your child the same feeling of support that he experiences in therapy. Consistency in both therapy and home allows for increased treatment progress. If this seems intimidating, think of it this way: you already used validating strategies when you approached your child about his self-injury and attempted to get him into treatment. You're practically an old pro at validation!

Just to review for a moment, validation means acknowledging your child's point of view without dismissing it, contradicting it, or minimizing it. Your child may express his emotions in regard to a variety of situations. Give him the opportunity to express his feelings, and acknowledge why it is understandable that he feels the way he does, given his life circumstance and his viewpoint. This applies not just to urges to cut but to general life circumstances as well. He may come home from school and express his sense of unfairness about a test or his anger toward a sibling. Responding with understanding and validation can help him with his recovery. Remember that self-injury can be a function of difficulty identifying and dealing with emotions in a variety of circumstances; giving him a safe environment in which to express himself is an integral component of his recovery. Expressing himself appropriately using words rather than hurting himself is probably one of the most important skills the therapist is trying to teach him. You can help by being the nonjudgmental person he can turn to during these times. Seeking you out may be one of the skills on his list of coping strategies.

Below is an example of how you might use validation.

Child: I can't do this! Therapy isn't going to work for me.

Parent: I can see it's difficult and I know how hard you're trying. You've made the effort to go to every appointment. What you're experiencing does take a lot of hard work and you will be frustrated at times. I know that you have the strength to hang in there.

What if I know my child just cut himself? Should I say anything?

You know your child just cut and you're worried about his emotional state and whether he might start doing it again on a regular basis. Should you get involved? This is an extremely tricky situation. We suggest that you discuss this during a therapy appointment with your child present. In general, adolescents don't want to talk about the cutting itself but may be more open to discussing the situation that is creating their emotional crisis. Offer to be a listening ear. Instead of saying, "I know you just cut. Did you use your therapy?" say something like this: "It seems like you are having a rough day. You seem to be struggling today and seem depressed [or angry, frustrated, or another feeling]. I'd love to try to help or just listen. Can I do anything for you?" In this way the focus is on the trigger leading him to cut rather than on the behavior itself. Discussing the behavior is likely to make your child defensive and shut down, since he already knows that he "shouldn't" be cutting. Focusing on the trigger and maybe teaching him how to use some problem-solving or coping skills in the moment is the ultimate goal anyway. If your child identifies his difficulty, try to break down the problem into concrete steps and help him decide on a reasonable solution.

The only exception to this suggestion is if you believe that your child has harmed himself seriously enough to require medical intervention. In that situation, don't be afraid to get him help no matter how you do it. The ramifications of your "interference" can be addressed in follow-up therapy sessions.

What if my child is not being truthful to the therapist?

Confronting your child about this will probably result in tension and frustration in your relationship. Therapists who are trained to deal with these kinds of difficulties are aware that, at times, it is hard for a patient to be truthful. The goal of the therapy then is to identify the reasons why your child may be holding back information. The therapist would probably approach the issue by first validating the fact that being honest about such a sensitive topic is a struggle for many people. The therapist would also refrain from accusing your child of deliberately sabotaging treatment or not wanting to get better. The therapist would convey the belief that your child is doing the best he can. He or she will remind your child what he has to gain from being truthful during therapy. Observing how your child's therapist validates him and how he or she deals with failures, conflict, dishonesty, and other difficult issues will provide you with a framework for dealing with these issues with your child outside of therapy. Mirroring the therapist's approach by listening to the tone and message he or she sends your child will help you to communicate more effectively with your child in general, especially when coping with his self-injury.

Following this approach will help your child through the process and hopefully become more truthful. If you are concerned that your child is holding back a significant amount of information, then finding an appropriate way to communicate this fact to the therapist, either through a phone call or note, is a valid solution.

What if my child refuses my involvement during any part of treatment?

We have seen some adolescents who refuse to involve their parents in treatment. Unfortunately, the more you push, the more your child will feel that his boundaries are being crossed. Take the opportunity, either during a therapy appointment or at a time when you have his attention, to communicate why it's important to you to be involved in his treatment. With the therapist's help, determine whether your request is reasonable. Obviously, requesting to sit in on every session or wanting to know exactly what was said during an appointment is not reasonable. It is, however, reasonable to request being present for ten to fifteen minutes every two to four weeks (assuming your child has weekly appointments) to be given a summary on your child's progress. Allow your child to express his reasons for denying the request in the first place, and attempt to negotiate to a level of involvement that is comfortable for your child. In the beginning, you may have to agree to have very limited contact with his therapist or receive very little information. But remember that some involvement is better than none. Once your child becomes comfortable with the current situation, you can slowly request additional time, information, and so on. If you have had a clear discussion about confidentiality rules in the early phase of treatment, then you know that the therapist is legally bound to inform you if your child is an imminent threat to himself or others. So if something really important comes up, the therapist will involve you in the situation.

Regardless of your child's level of comfort with your involvement, we suggest that you become familiar with the therapy approach and therapeutic skills. The more familiar you are with the treatment, the easier it will be for you to have a dialogue with your child in the future. If your child senses that you really understand what is going on, he may be more willing to share his experience with you.

What if my child is involving me too much in treatment?

We have also come across situations in which the adolescent relies on his parent(s) to do the treatment for him. He may refuse to sit through an appointment alone, rely on his parents to answer the therapist's questions, or approach his parents with emotional crises and urges on a regular basis and insist that his parents resolve the issue for him. If you're a parent in this situation, you will quickly begin to feel overwhelmed, exhausted, and overinvolved. After all, your child is the one engaging in this behavior and he needs to take the responsibility for changing it. Setting limits will help him set similar boundaries in other relationships in his life.

Addressing this issue during a therapy session, with the aid of the therapist, is probably the most productive way to work through the issue. The first thing you address may be your level of involvement in the therapy session itself. You may have to negotiate concrete limits ("I will agree to sit through twenty minutes of your session," for example) and offer praise and rewards for his ability to follow through on the agreement.

Deciding on what limits to set at home, when your child may approach you too often for help with urges to self-injure, is much more difficult than negotiating limits on your presence in therapy sessions. How do you turn your child away if he is clearly seeking help for a behavior that you're all determined to get rid of? Well, the first question to ask is whether the manner in which your child approaches you is healthy and consistent with the therapy. Does he always use you as a strategy and refuse to implement any other skills? Does he cut if you're not immediately available rather than trying another strategy instead? Does he insist that it is your responsibility to take his pain away or that you are responsible for his suffering? If you've answered yes to these questions, then that would indicate that the issue needs to be addressed, because your child is having difficulty setting boundaries. Again, the most appropriate place to have this discussion is during an appointment.

If your child refuses to address the issue and it is clearly an ongoing struggle, then set aside some sessions just for yourself. Your child's therapist may not feel comfortable acting as your therapist if you need long-term support, so if that is the case you should ask for a referral to someone within the same treatment center or someone familiar with self-injury. In fact, it is a perfectly normal reaction to feel overwhelmed even if your child's requests are appropriate. Feeling that you have to say the right thing while your child is in crisis causes a large amount of strain in parents.

The therapist can coach you on how to communicate your boundaries to your child. You will need to let your child know that you care, that you want to help, and that you are more than willing to coach him through a crisis or self-injury urge, but that you and he will need to abide by certain rules with regard to the coaching sessions. Negotiate a contract with your child that involves compromise on both your parts. Agree to help if your child is willing to incorporate other strategies into his repertoire, if he agrees to try at least two other strategies if you are not available, and if he is able to seek your help in a respectful manner. Expecting him to be calm and reasonable is probably unlikely, but you can certainly request that he not be overly rude and disrespectful.

How do I maintain a dialogue with my child?

Maintaining a regular dialogue with your child means finding the proper balance between respecting your child's need for privacy and legitimately evaluating his progress. The behavior he is engaging in is highly volatile and unsafe. Staying out of the therapy process is just too frightening for many parents, who need some sense of how their child is progressing in treatment. Parents we have worked with say that the car ride to the therapy session often gives them the perfect opportunity to have a productive conversation with their child. If the conversation ends up in a disagreement, at least you have that therapy appointment in which to work through the issue!

In order to maintain an ongoing dialogue with your child you will have to work on developing a relationship and environment that is conducive to these kinds of conversations. That means respecting the limits he requests during joint therapy sessions and terminating a conversation when he requests it.

If you see him struggling with urges, focus on the reasons why he is having a hard time, in a nonjudgmental manner. If he has cut recently, stay positive. Communicate your belief that he has the potential to change rather than showing him that you are discouraged. Your child may feel despair and guilt every time he cuts. He may feel that he has disappointed his therapist and/or parents and that he will never get control of this behavior. He will turn to you to hear you give him reasons why this is not the case. Let him know that you believe in him and know that he has the strength to overcome this. Tell him that he is doing his best and that the reason he may be struggling is that he is simply learning and practicing new skills; knowing this will help him understand that he is not at fault. Reiterating that he has the potential to learn new skills will make him feel in control again.

How often do I mention the self-injury?

Once your child is in treatment, it is tempting to try to have frequent conversations with him about the self-injury. Remember that he is more than his cutting, so spend much of your time having "normal," everyday conversations like you've always done. Maintain as much normalcy and stability as possible. He needs to know that you haven't changed how you feel about him and to be reminded that he is not his illness—he is a person who happens to be suffering with an illness. Allow him privacy and the control to discuss the issue when he wants to. If he brings up the topic first, then by all means continue the conversation. However, it is best to avoid giving constant advice or feedback on skills you believe he should be using. Instead, an occasional passing comment, made at an appropriate time, praising him for his effort and commitment to treatment will go a long way.

What can I do for myself?

With so much of your time and energy spent recently finding a therapist, driving your child to and from his appointments, worrying about his well-being, and negotiating all of your other daily demands, we'd be surprised if you weren't exhausted and stressed. All of the time you have invested researching, reading, and planning how to approach your child has probably left you with little time or energy for yourself, not to mention the emotional strain that this must be causing. Taking care of yourself, as obvious as that is, can be forgotten among all of the recent crises you've been dealing with. We echo all of the other self-help books by reminding you to take time out to engage in pleasurable activities. Invest even half an hour a day doing something that relaxes and rejuvenates you.

At times of crisis, many people really want to reach out to their friends for support. But it is sometimes hard for parents to discuss their child's self-injury with their friends, since the topic can cause a lot of discomfort and people often don't know how to respond. If you are not getting the emotional support you need within your existing social circle, then seek your own therapy, even if only to have a place to go where someone understands what you are going through. Seek out support groups for parents if they exist in your area. Ask your child's therapist if he or she knows parents who may be willing to talk to you. The Internet can also be a way to find other parents going through similar situations. We find that having an outlet to discuss feelings and concerns can be a good source of comfort.

10

Specific Skills to Use at Home: Name It, Tame It, Break It Down

One of the most stressful situations for parents is when a child approaches them with an urge to cut while at home or out in public. Most parents worry about doing or saying the wrong thing in such a scenario, because they think that one false move can make the difference between their child's safety and self-injury. In this chapter we offer a few simple skills that can help you get your child (and yourself) through her urge to cut with little more than white knuckles.

Let's start with how to respond. First, don't panic. We know you want to, but try to stay calm. Even if you have to "fake it 'til you make it" by talking a good game, doing so will help your child keep from escalating emotionally. If she senses that you're in control, then she will be more likely to stay in control. Sure, your legs might feel like they're made of jelly and your heart is probably racing like a freight train, but you can handle this. You've almost made it to the end of our book. You're practically an expert.

Child: Mom, I want to cut myself right now!

Parent: (to self) Oh my God! Oh my God! What the hell do I do?

Parent: (to child) Okay, let's take it slowly and follow the plan that you've been using in therapy.

If your child has sought you out, consider your relationship with her and her therapy thus far a success. This means she's using one of her strategies. Remember, it is not your sole responsibility to prevent your child from cutting in that moment. Let's face it—she's going to do it if she wants to. It is only your job to be a pillar for her and to help her to use her skills.

To assist our patients in remembering how to handle a crisis situation, we have devised an easy rhyme: "Name it, tame it, break it down." You can also use this in your discussions with your child, to help you both remain calm and focused. We know it's corny, but you'll see that it really works.

Most of the techniques that we have developed here are adaptations of basic techniques from dialectical behavior therapy (Linehan 1993b), modified to suit children and adolescents. These are the same techniques we use with our own patients in therapy, adapted for at-home use. We also recommend that you ask your child's therapist if he or she has any handouts or flashcards that might be helpful for use at home.

NAME IT: FIGURING OUT WHAT YOU'RE FEELING

Naming, or identifying, the emotion that your child is experiencing at the moment she has the urge to cut will help both you and her to understand what is driving that urge. Remember, most self-injury is emotion-driven behavior. If you can help your child to successfully identify exactly what emotion is fueling her self-injury flame, you will be able to help her control it.

When your child comes to you with an urge to cut, try not to figure out why or engage in a lengthy logical discussion about what set her off. She cannot have that discussion at the moment. Her emotional state is too intense and she will simply become even more frustrated. Instead, have a very simple and brief talk to help her identify her feelings. Sometimes, simply allowing her to talk and express herself will be the most important way you can help.

Generally, when your child is at the point where she wants to cut herself, she's already caught in a vortex of negative emotion. When you first question her about how she feels, she might say, "I feel horrible! What do you think?!" Encourage her to be a little more specific. You can help her by engaging her in a quick dialogue like this:

Parent: Look, I know you feel really bad right now, but let's try to figure out exactly what kind of bad feeling you're having so we can help you get through it better. Okay?

Child: I feel really messed up and kind of numb.

Parent: Okay, you're feeling numb. I understand that. Anything else? Are you feeling sad, worried, angry, embarrassed?

Child: Yeah, I was feeling really angry because my friends all ditched me. Then I started to feel numb, like out of my body.

Parent: So you're also dissociating?

Child: Yes. Mom, can you help me?

Parent: Totally.

Sometimes, it's not this easy; other times it is. If your child is having a really hard time, try to get her to commit to first more general categories, and then to specific feelings. If she can get more specific and is able to pinpoint the level of intensity of a particular emotion, encourage her to do this, using the following table.

In DBT, clients learn to identify their emotions (Linehan 1993b). In our experience, adolescents often find it difficult to identify specific feelings, so we've designed this table to help them not only identify specific feelings but also to break them into general categories with levels of intensity so they can understand the relationship between particular feelings. The table is broken down by category (agitated, subdued, shameful), then further by class of feelings (angry, sad, and so on), and then even further by examples of specific feelings in order of intensity (for example, low-intensity anger is called "annoyed," moderate-intensity anger is referred to as "mad," and high-intensity anger is labeled as "enraged").

Agitated	Subdued	Shameful
Angry feelings	**Sad feelings**	**Embarrassed feelings**
Annoyed	Down	Self-conscious
Mad	Depressed	Embarrassed
Enraged	Despondent	Mortified
Anxious feelings	**Numb feelings**	**Jealous feelings**
Worried	Detached	Resentful
Anxious	Disconnected	Envious
Terrified	Dissociated	Jealous
Overwhelmed feelings	**Bored feelings**	**Ashamed feelings**
Concerned	Indifferent	Guilty
Stressed out	Apathetic	Ashamed
Overwhelmed	Bored	Humiliated

Once your child has named her specific feelings, validate her and let her know that you are there for her. The hard part, once you've helped your child identify what she's feeling, is helping her to ride out those emotions. The next section is designed to provide you and your child with some strategies to experience her difficult feelings without becoming overwhelmed by them. We affectionately refer to this as "feeling and dealing," or "taming" the difficult emotions.

TAME IT: HOW TO TONE DOWN INTENSE EMOTIONS

So now you and your child have pinpointed how she's feeling. You're halfway to helping her through the urge. The next step is to help your child find a specific strategy to cope with the emotion and the urge. Sometimes, experiencing an intense emotion head-on is almost intolerable (and is in fact the most common reason why individuals self-injure). Your child may be perceiving her emotion as dangerous and be afraid to feel it, because she is associating it with the urge to cut. We usually respond to this fear by telling our patients, "There is no such thing as a dangerous emotion. There is only dangerous behavior." Avoidance of emotions just keeps you running and makes you more vulnerable to repeated intense experiences of those feelings.

Sometimes, toning down an intense emotion can help your child to tolerate experiencing it. Some good rules of thumb that we use in our own treatment and teach to our patients are the following: (1) substitute intensity for injury by experiencing intense sensations that are safe, and (2) ease your way out of uncomfortable feelings by soothing your senses.

Below are emotion regulation strategies based on basic DBT protocol (Linehan 1993b). However, we've modified them so they're more accessible to younger teens and even children, to encourage them to find specific behavioral strategies that help them tame their fierce feelings.

At a time when your child is not having an urge, you might want to have her make a list of activities that she knows are either intense or soothing, so that she has an arsenal of her own tried-and-true coping strategies to turn to. Some suggestions for safe yet intense activities and sensations include the following:

- Holding ice

- Throwing eggs or apples at trees (Don't aim at people or squirrels.)

- Jumping on a trampoline until exhausted

- Sticking your face in a basin of ice water

- Sucking on a lemon

- Screaming at the top of your lungs (Warn others that you will be doing this, or scream into a pillow.)

Some of the more soothing suggestions that our patients like include the following:

- Taking a bath

- Taking a walk near a river or ocean beach or listening to the sounds of nature

- Using a chilled gel-filled eye mask

- Lighting scented candles, or using incense or essential oils of lavender or peppermint

- Chilling a favorite body lotion in the fridge, then slathering it on after a shower or bath

- Playing with a pet

Some other DBT-based strategies (Linehan 1993b) that we recommend include engaging in a healthy but distracting activity while allowing oneself to experience feelings (riding a bike while feeling angry until the feeling begins to fade) and doing something to find the meaning in the situation (helping your child to focus on how much better she's dealing with her feelings than she was last year, or trying to focus on her good choices thus far, like telling you she had an urge and asking for help instead of cutting).

Help your child determine whether she needs to experience an intense sensory experience, self-soothe, distract herself, or try to find some meaning in the situation. Validate her emotions and then let her use the conversation with you to arrive at ways that she can experience her emotions by coping with them safely and effectively, while riding out her urge to cut. Of course, if at any time you think that you are in over your head, call her therapist. Like most therapists who treat self-injuring children and teens, we try to be very available to our patients, so when difficult circumstances arise, and they've tried to apply their skills but are having trouble, we are there to help them continue to resist injuring until the urge has passed. (However, individual practices may vary, so it is best to discuss your therapist's preferences for handling off-hours phone calls at the outset of therapy.)

BREAK IT DOWN: FUNCTIONAL BEHAVIOR ASSESSMENT YOU CAN DO AT HOME

Once the urge is past and your child is safe, you can take some time and talk over exactly what triggered the urge, why it happened, and what she liked or didn't like about how she coped. Trying to do this while your child is still very emotional, or while she is at the height of an urge, is not advisable. It's like trying to reason with someone who is drunk. It would be frustrating for both of you and might lead your child to avoid seeking you out next time she's in crisis. But if you are patient and wait until the timing is better, you will both learn more from this exercise.

Successfully "breaking it down" has a lot to do with asking the right questions.

What was the trigger?

First, begin by identifying the trigger. Triggers are antecedent events, people, situations, feelings, memories—anything that your child experienced or was involved in immediately before she developed the urge to self-injure. Below are some questions that you can ask that will help your child to identify her triggers:

- Where were you when you got the urge?

- Who were you with?

- What was going on?

- What were you doing?

What was that feeling again?

Once you have established what led to your child's urge to cut, take a minute to reflect on the feelings that your child identified previously to help her begin to identify the link between her feelings and her behaviors. Since she already identified her feelings with you in the moment, reflect back on what she said and identify those specific feelings (in this case it was angry and numb; see the section "Name It" above) as potential emotional precursors to cutting. That way, if she knows what feelings lead to her self-destructive urges, and she knows what specific situations trigger these feelings, she will be much wiser in the future when history repeats itself.

What made you more vulnerable?

Sometimes, even being aware of one's feelings and situational triggers doesn't prevent self-injurious urges from happening. At certain times and under certain circumstances we are all more or less vulnerable to certain negative emotions and behavioral urges. For example, we all know that the wrong time to go food shopping is when we are tired and hungry, right? Well, self-injury is no different from any other impulsive behavior (like buying chips, toaster pastries, and a pint of rocky road ice cream when all we really needed was shaving cream and a box of cereal). It's important to help your child identify what made her vulnerable. Any aversive physiological state (like illness, pain, lack of sleep, fatigue, hunger) or psychological state (anger, anxiety, depression, acute stressors, ongoing stressors) can reduce our natural coping abilities and may make us more prone to slipping back into older, maladaptive patterns of behavior, or at least craving them.

One vulnerability that we would be remiss not to mention, and one that fits into both the physiological and psychological categories, is premenstrual syndrome (PMS). Though this may not seem like an important variable in dealing with self-injurious urges, PMS can definitely affect one's ability to cope with vulnerability and intense emotions. PMS occurs when estrogen bottoms out in the week before menstruation. Estrogen facilitates serotonin transmission (there's that pesky neurotransmitter again), so when estrogen's low, serotonin isn't traveling around in the brain with maximum efficiency. Since serotonin is the brain chemical associated with mood, anxiety, sleep, appetite, and practically everything else in the body, it makes sense that PMS would lead an individual to have difficulties regulating these functions. Many women who cut report increased vulnerability to self-injury urges in the week before their menstrual period begins. To find out if this is an issue for your daughter, track her cycles on a calendar simply by noting the first day of her last period each month and by having her rate her mood and self-injurious urges each day.

Knowing your child's vulnerabilities can help you to help her when she comes to you with an urge. Encouraging your child to also be aware of her vulnerabilities will help her keep herself on top of her emotional game, so to speak, so that she understands why she may be feeling more negative, depressed, angry, or anxious and doesn't get blindsided by these feelings.

What were you thinking?

We ask our kids this question all the time. But in this case, the goal is really to work with whatever they give you. It is important to work with your child to help her to identify any negative or extreme thinking that might have led to her negative emotional experiences. As we demonstrated in the section on cognitive behavioral therapy, extreme thinking leads to extreme feelings. Help your child to make this link between her thoughts and emotions by identifying negative thinking and then restructuring it with her to make it sound a little more moderate. Then have her try it on for size and see how it feels, compared to the higher-intensity thinking she was previously engaging in. Below are some ways to seek and destroy irrational thinking. This list is certainly not exhaustive, but it demonstrates some common cognitive errors and how to correct them.

- Black-and-white thinking

  - Catch phrases: "I always . . ." "You never . . ." "It's completely . . ."

  - Change to gray thinking: "I sometimes . . ." "Lately you haven't . . ." "It's somewhat . . ."

- Demands

  - Catch phrases: "I should." "I must." "I have to."

  - Change to preferences: "I want to." "I'd like to." "I'd prefer to."

- Can'ts

  - Catch phrases: "I can't stand it!" "I can't handle it!" "I can't tolerate it!"

- Change to coping: "I don't like it, but I can stand it." "This sucks, but I can handle it for a while." "I really don't like this, but I can tolerate it."

■ Rating self and others

- Catch phrases: "He's an idiot for thinking that!" "I'm a failure at life because I failed my test!" "She's a total bitch for saying that!"

- Change to: "His opinion may be idiotic, but I can't judge him by that alone." "I'm really bummed about failing my test, but there are things I do well on, too." "That comment was really bitchy, but she's said some stuff that's not so bad."

■ Perfectionism

- Catch phrases: "I have to be the best!" "I need 100 on this test!" "I have to look perfect today!"

- Change to realism: "I'd like to do my best, but if I don't, it doesn't mean I'm the worst." "I want 100 on this test, but if I get something above an 85, I guess it will be decent enough." "I want to look nice today."

How did you do?

At this point, you can look back with your child on the whole episode from start to finish and examine how both you and she handled the situation. Encourage her to focus on her choices that she liked as well as those that she didn't like. Ask her what she might choose to do differently the next time around. Have your child articulate the skills that she used, as well as what you did that worked or didn't work. By doing this, you'll continue to improve the ways both you and your child handle self-injurious urges as they come up. Eventually, if you're implementing the effective skills consistently, the frequency, intensity, and even the duration of the urges will likely begin to dwindle.

APPENDIX

Frequently Asked Questions

1. *What is self-injurious behavior?* It is a direct, intentional, repetitive behavior resulting in mild to moderate physical injury.

2. *What types of self-injurious behaviors are there?* There are many ways to hurt oneself, but the most common are cutting, burning, scratching, skin picking, nail biting to the point of bleeding, and head banging.

3. *What are the usual signs to look for?* If your child shows a change in mood, acts moody, avoids wearing clothes that might expose certain areas of the body, avoids certain activities like swimming, carries around sharp implements such as tweezers and razors, makes excuses for bruises and scratches, is withdrawing, is more secretive, and has frequent conflicts with friends, then your child may be engaging in self-injury.

4. *Are the behaviors actually attempts at committing suicide?* Not typically. Most of the time the intent of the act is to help the person cope with negative emotions or to control the immediate environment rather than to die. Accidental death can occur in certain circumstances. Suicidal thoughts are often experienced by individuals who self-injure.

5. *Does it ever result in suicide?* Yes, approximately 10 percent of self-injurers complete suicide.

6. *What percentage actually engage in suicide at some point unrelated to the self-injurious behavior?* Approximately 50 percent to 90 percent engage in suicidal behavior.

7. *Are there different types of self-injury?* Yes, there are four different types: impulsive, major, stereotypic, and compulsive.

8. *Why would anyone purposefully hurt him- or herself?* There are different reasons for the different types of self-injurious behaviors. For example, in the impulsive type the behavior might be a way to deal with loneliness, poor interpersonal relations, feelings of emptiness, or negative emotions; in the major type it may be due to a psychotic or manic episode or drug intoxication; in the stereotypic type it is related to autism, Prader-Willi, or mental retardation; and in the compulsive type it may be due to Tourette's syndrome, body dysmorphic disorder, or trichotillomania.

9. *Who is more likely to engage in self-injurious behavior—males or females?* Mainly females, but some males also engage in self-injury.

10. *What percentage of the population is actually affected?* Anywhere from 1 percent to 4 percent. It is estimated that approximately 3 million Americans engage in self-injury.

11. *At what age does it typically begin?* Usually around age fourteen to sixteen, but it can continue into the fifties.

12. *Is there a specific group of people who are more likely to self-injure?* Yes. Researchers have found that people who have been abused, have borderline personality disorder, suffer from poor body image, and suffer from eating disorders are more likely to self-injure.

13. *Is it manipulative behavior to get attention?* No, the person is really suffering. Neither over- nor under-responding will make the problem go away.

14. *Isn't it painful?* Sometimes, but not always. In fact, some people report feeling almost nothing before and during cutting, while others report diminished pain accompanied by a rush, a feeling of relief, or even euphoria.

15. *Are self-injurers aware of what they are doing?* They may be in a state of dissociation when they begin to cut, and then they become aware of their body and self as they proceed to cut. The desire to feel and be alive is often the reason they are doing it.

16. *On what part of the body do they typically self-injure?* It can involve any part of the body but is typically done on the wrists, arms, legs, breasts, chest, and abdomen.

17. *How often do they usually engage in the behavior?* The frequency varies from person to person—anywhere from several times a day to once every few months.

18. *Does it become more dangerous the more frequently they hurt themselves?* Not really, but you only need to hurt yourself severely once to produce irreversible results. Obviously, you increase your chances the more times you engage in the behavior.

19. *What should I do if I suspect that my loved one is self-injuring?* Talk to her. Find out what triggers the self-injury. Get the proper professional help.

20. *What are the usual triggers?* Any life stressor can be a trigger. Usually self-injury is triggered by dealing with painful emotions, romantic breakups, starting college, feeling rejected, and abuse.

21. *What does abuse have to do with self-injury?* Research has shown that those who have been sexually abused tend to cut more often than others. This is also true of people who have eating disorders. A person who has been abused usually loathes his or her body.

22. *Is there a biological basis for this behavior?* Research suggests there may be.

23. *What are the biological bases?* Several theories have been put forth, including the serotonin theory, the endogenous opiate hypothesis, and the cortisol and norepinephrine theory.

24. *What is the serotonin theory?* Serotonin is a substance in our body that regulates irritability, depression, suicidality, and compulsivity. Because these symptoms are linked to self-injury, it is believed that serotonin may be too low in individuals who self-injure.

25. *What is the endogenous opiate hypothesis?* Endogenous opiates, or endorphins, are substances in our body that act like an opiate and may be too low in some people. The act of self-injury may restore them to normal levels.

26. *What is the cortisol and norepinephrine theory?* Both cortisol and norepinephrine are secreted by the adrenal gland and regulate our reaction to stress. Cortisol levels may be too low in self-injurers. Under stress, when the levels generally increase, self-injurers are very sensitive to the change. For this reason, they do not respond well to stress. On the other hand, norepinephrine levels may be too high and this may cause impulsivity and aggression.

27. *Is self-injurious behavior addictive?* Chronic overstimulation of endorphins may lead to an increase in tolerance of the opiate response and an increased need to self-injure. An endorphin "rush" occurs in self-injurers, which leads to feelings of relief and relaxation.

28. *Can someone become immediately addicted?* Some researchers have suggested that somewhere between the twentieth or thirtieth cut the act may become addictive.

29. *Are self-injurers in pain when they cut?* The hypothesis regarding pain suggests that dysregulation of the endogenous opiate system leads to decreased pain responsivity (the reason self-injurers need to cut more frequently and intensely over time, and why marked anesthesia seems to be present in some cutters). In turn, this leads to the increased likelihood of dissociation, which can only be broken by self-injury. These would be described as the individuals who "cut to feel."

30. *What role does our society play in promoting self-injury?* There are various environmental influences, including family factors, the media, and peer influences.

31. *Isn't it true that there is more body piercing in the Western world than in other cultures?* Yes, that is true.

32. *Are body piercing and tattooing forms of self-injury?* No, they are not, by our definition. Self-injury has to be an intentional and direct infliction of self-harm that interferes with functioning.

33. *Is it ever all right to self-injure?* Certain cultures have engaged in collective self-injurious behavior as an expression of repent, mourning, or beautification. However, these are rituals that the society sanctions, and their intent is not to harm.

34. *How is that different from someone doing it alone?* When it is performed alone and not for a culturally sanctioned reason, it is socially unacceptable. This response to stress, negative affect, or upset is maladaptive and eventually leads to impairment in functioning.

35. *Can a person actually learn to self-injure from others?* Yes. It's possible to learn to imitate a self-injurer. However, unless you have a biological predisposition, it would be just an experiment and would probably not become an ongoing behavior.

36. *Is there any way to tell whether one has a predisposition if the behavior has just begun?* Clinically, it seems that those who are biologically predisposed do not experience as much pain when they cut initially.

37. *Is the media a contributor?* Yes and no. If one has the biological and psychological predisposition to self-injure, then the answer would be yes.

38. *If my child is listening to certain music with lyrics about cutting, should I be concerned?* A single behavior in isolation isn't likely to mean anything. Look for a combination of different signs mentioned in this book. As with everything else, it is best to talk to your child rather than ignore certain behaviors. Inquire what your child thinks about the music, and the idea of cutting. Ask whether he knows anyone who cuts, and what he thinks about it.

39. *What could happen physically if my child engaged in self-injury?* Physical consequences are many, including infection, scarring, bleeding to the point of anemia, and death.

40. *Should I take my child to the emergency room if I see a cut?* You need to seek help but not necessarily go to the emergency room. The right response depends on many factors.

41. *When would I go to the emergency room?* You would only go to the emergency room if your child were bleeding badly, if the cut were pretty deep, or if your child were suicidal.

42. *When should hospitalization be considered?* Hospitalization is necessary if your child is suicidal, cannot stop cutting even for a day, and engages in other maladaptive behaviors, like starvation, drug usage, and so on.

43. *How do I assess for suicidality?* Using the acronym SLAP, assess for specificity of the suicide plan, lethality of means, availability of resources to carry out the plan, and proximity of any supportive person.

44. *What do you mean by "specificity"?* Determine how clear, detailed, and specific the suicidal plan is. The more detailed and well thought out the plan is, the greater the degree of risk.

45. *What do you mean by "lethality of means"?* How dangerous is the method she plans to use? What are the chances of death based on the method she has in mind?

46. *What does "availability of resources" mean?* Determine whether the method he has chosen is available to him (such as a gun, carbon monoxide, or hanging).

47. *What do you mean by "proximity of supportive family"?* Proximity refers to the availability of supportive people in your child's life. Is your child living alone or does she live with you? Has your family just moved to a new town where you don't know anyone, or does your family have a well-developed support network, having lived in your town for many years?

48. *What if I think he is suicidal—then what?* Take him immediately to a hospital. Call your child's therapist and psychiatrist, if he is already working with one.

49. *Should I take her alone?* It is best to have at least two adults present, if only to have someone to keep your child safe on the way to the hospital.

50. *What if my child refuses to go?* Call 911 or the mobile crisis unit in your area.

51. *What is a mobile crisis unit?* It is a group of professionals who will come to your house to determine the seriousness of the situation and will take your child to the hospital if necessary.

52. *How do I get information about the mobile crisis unit?* Every county has one. Call your local department of health for the number. Keep it handy.

53. *If my child is admitted to the hospital, what will the staff do for him?* Most likely they will give medication and monitor the child for a while to make sure he is safe. Hospitalization is a short-term solution. Your child will need outpatient therapy immediately afterward.

54. *Is it all right if I have a professional talk to my child, instead of talking to my child myself?* No, it is not. It is important that you first approach your child (this is assuming you are not on your way to the hospital). After you have spoken to your child about the self-injury and why she may be engaging in this dangerous behavior, then it is advisable to take your child to a professional who is familiar with self-injury. Otherwise, your child may perceive that you are disinterested or too uncomfortable with the behavior to deal with her.

55. *How will I know that the professional is knowledgeable?* Ask the person how many self-injurers they have treated, what treatment method they use, and whether you will be involved. Be sure to get specific answers.

56. *What happens if my child doesn't want to talk about it when I approach him?* The likelihood is that your child will be uncomfortable discussing self-injury with you, deny it, make excuses, or make promises to stop. You may have to pursue the topic. Pick the right time and location to have the discussion. Validate your child and respect his boundaries, but be persistent and patient.

57. *What happens if my child walks away or is angry?* Stay calm and empathize—you too would feel annoyed if someone were asking you these types of questions. Express why you are concerned and that although it is difficult for both of you, it is important that you talk about it.

58. *What happens if my child just turns it around and says I am totally wrong?* You must present your child with what you have observed in her behavior that is concerning you. Stay away from discussing your own needs or opinions.

59. *What are the most important things to emphasize?* First, validate how uncomfortable it is to talk about this subject, and then describe the behavior, express care and concern, and encourage the conversation.

60. *What do I do if my child still refuses?* Tell your child you will not bring up the issue for a week, allowing time to think it over, and then seriously do not bring it up until that week is out. You may have to do this a few times.

61. *What if each time he refuses to talk?* Offer him a therapist to talk to. Tell your child that he can discuss things confidentially with the therapist.

62. *What if she gives an excuse and denies it?* Denial and excuses are the same as not talking. Present the facts—describe what you have observed. Be persistent and patient.

63. *Should I give my child materials on self-injury? Would it help?* By all means, provide information that you have collected. This may also help your child open up.

64. *What is the appropriate treatment?* It is cognitive behavioral therapy (CBT), or a form of CBT called dialectical behavior therapy (DBT).

65. *What is CBT?* It is a treatment method based on learning how to change your thoughts and behaviors in order to better cope with stressors. It teaches you specific strategies to change your thoughts, values, and attitudes and how to act differently in various situations.

66. *What is DBT?* It is a variant of CBT. DBT teaches the individual to find a balance between his extreme perspective and that of others. It teaches the person to regulate his emotions.

67. *What are some of the things my child will learn with DBT?* She will learn skills for problem solving, emotion regulation, mindfulness, and distress tolerance, and how to enhance relationships.

68. *What is mindfulness?* It is a form of contemplation or meditation in which the individual stays in the present and participates in life with awareness.

69. *What can I do to stay involved in my child's treatment?* Meet regularly with the therapist, respect your child's boundaries, educate yourself about self-injury and its treatment, and facilitate regular conversations with your child.

70. *What if my child comes to me with an urge to self-injure?* Encourage your child to use the skills learned in therapy. Be supportive. Don't panic. Analyze the triggering event after the situation has passed. If you think you need backup, encourage your child to call his therapist.

References

Alexander, C. 2003. *The Bounty*. New York: Penguin Group (USA) Inc.

American Psychiatric Association. 1994. *Diagnostic and Statistical Manual of Mental Disorders (DSM-IV)*. 4th ed. Washington, DC: American Psychiatric Association.

Briere, J., and E. Gil. 1998. Self-mutilation in clinical and general population samples: Prevalence, correlates, and functions. *American Journal of Orthopsychiatry* 68(4):609–20.

DiClemente, R., L. Ponton, and D. Hartley. 1991. Prevalence and correlates of cutting behavior: Risk for HIV transmission. *Journal of the American Academy of Child and Adolescent Psychiatry* 30(5):735–39.

Favazza, A. 1998. The coming of age of self-mutilation. *Journal of Nervous and Mental Disease* 186(5):259–68.

Favazza, A., and K. Conterio. 1989. Female habitual self-mutilators. *Acta Psychiatrica Scandinavica* 79:282–89.

Gardner, A. R., and A. J. Gardner. 1975. Self-mutilation, obsessionality and narcissism. *British Journal of Psychiatry* 127:127–32.

Greenberg, P. E., R. C. Kessler, H. G. Birnbaum, S. A. Leong, S. W. Lowe, P. A. Berglund, and P. K. Corey-Lisle. 2003. The economic burden of depression in the United States: How did it change between 1990 and 2000. *Journal of Clinical Psychiatry* 64:1465-1475.

Herpertz, S., H. Sass, and A. Favazza. 1997. Impulsivity in self-mutilative behavior: Psychometric and biological findings. *Journal of Psychiatric Research* 31(4):451–65.

Koda, H. 2001. *Extreme Beauty: The Body Transformed.* New York: Metropolitan Museum of Art.

Linehan, M. M. 1993a. *Cognitive-Behavioral Treatment of Borderline Personality Disorder.* New York: Guilford Press.

———. 1993b. *Skills Training Manual for Treating Borderline Personality Disorder.* New York: Guilford Press.

McKay, D., S. Kulchycky, and S. Danyko. 2000. Borderline personality and obsessive-compulsive symptoms. *Journal of Personality Disorders* 14(1):57–63.

Miller, P. H. 1985. *Information Center: Training Workshop Manual.* San Diego: Information Center.

New, A., R. Trestman, V. Mitropoulou, D. Benishay, E. Coccaro, J. Silverman, and L. Siever. 1997. Serotonergic function and self-injurious behavior in personality disorder patients. *Psychiatry Research* 69:17–26.

Oquendo, M., and J. Mann. 2000. The biology of impulsivity and suicidality. *Psychiatric Clinics of North America* 23(1):11–24.

Pattison, E., and J. Kahan. 1983. The deliberate self-harm syndrome. *American Journal of Psychiatry* 140:867–72.

Rodriguez-Srednicki, O. 2001. Childhood sexual abuse, dissociation, and adult self-destructive behavior. *Journal of Child Sexual Abuse* 10(3):75–90.

Ross, S., and N. Heath. 2002. A study of the frequency of self-mutilation in a community sample of adolescents. *Journal of Youth and Adolescence* 31(1):67–77.

Russ, M. 1992. Self-injurious behavior in patients with borderline personality disorder: Biological perspectives. *Journal of Personality Disorders* 6:64–81.

Sachsse, U., S. Von Der Heyde, and G. Huether. 2002. Stress regulation and self-mutilation. *American Journal of Psychiatry* 159(4):672.

Sansone, R., G. Gaither, and D. Songer. 2002. Self-harm behaviors across the life cycle: A pilot study of inpatients with borderline personality disorder. *Comprehensive Psychiatry* 43(3):215–18.

Simeon, D., B. Stanley, and A. J. Frances. 1992. Self-mutilation in personality disorders: Psychological and biological correlates. *American Journal of Psychiatry* 149(2):221–26.

Suyemoto, K. 1998. The functions of self-mutilation. *Clinical Psychology Review* 18(5):531–54.

Winchel, R., and M. Stanley. 1991. Self-injurious behavior: A review of the behavior and biology of self-mutilation. *American Journal of Psychiatry* 148:306–17.

Merry E. McVey-Noble, Ph.D., is a psychologist at the Bio-Behavioral Institute in Great Neck, NY, where she treats a number of adolescents and adults who engage in self-injurious behaviors. She is adjunct professor of psychology at Hofstra University, where she has taught for ten years.

Sony Khemlani-Patel, Ph.D., is a licensed clinical psychologist at the Bio-Behavioral Institute in Great Neck, NY, where she specializes in the treatment and research of obsessive-compulsive spectrum, anxiety, and mood disorders as well as self-injury. She received her doctorate from Hofstra University in Hempstead, NY.

Fugen Neziroglu, Ph.D., ABBP, is a board-certified cognitive and behavior psychologist, involved in the research and treatment of anxiety disorders, obsessive-compulsive spectrum disorders, trichotillomania, hoarding, body dysmorphic disorder, and hypochondriasis at the Bio-Behavioral Institute in Great Neck, NY. She is coauthor of **Overcoming Compulsive Hoarding.**

Some Other
New Harbinger Titles

Helping A Child with Nonverbal Learning Disorder, 2nd edition
Item 5266 $15.95

The Introvert & Extrovert in Love, Item 4863 $14.95

Helping Your Socially Vulnerable Child, Item 4580 $15.95

Life Planning for Adults with Developmental Disabilities, Item 4511 $19.95

But I Didn't Mean That! Item 4887 $14.95

The Family Intervention Guide to Mental Illness, Item 5068 $17.95

It's So Hard to Love You, Item 4962 $14.95

The Turbulent Twenties, Item 4216 $14.95

The Balanced Mom, Item 4534 $14.95

Helping Your Child Overcome Separation Anxiety & School Refusal,
Item 4313 $14.95

When Your Child Is Cutting, Item 4375 $15.95

Helping Your Child with Selective Mutism, Item 416X $14.95

Sun Protection for Life, Item 4194 $11.95

Helping Your Child with Autism Spectrum Disorder, Item 3848 $17.95

Teach Me to Say It Right, Item 4038 $13.95

Grieving Mindfully, Item 4011 $14.95

The Courage to Trust, Item 3805 $14.95

The Gift of ADHD, Item 3899 $14.95

The Power of Two Workbook, Item 3341 $19.95

Adult Children of Divorce, Item 3368 $14.95

*Fifty Great Tips, Tricks, and Techniques to Connect
with Your Teen,* Item 3597 $10.95

Helping Your Child with OCD, Item 3325 $19.95

Helping Your Depressed Child, Item 3228 $14.95

Call **toll free, 1-800-748-6273,** or log on to our online bookstore at **www.newharbinger.com** to order. Have your Visa or Mastercard number ready. Or send a check for the titles you want to New Harbinger Publications, Inc., 5674 Shattuck Ave., Oakland, CA 94609. Include $4.50 for the first book and 75¢ for each additional book, to cover shipping and handling. (California residents please include appropriate sales tax.) Allow two to five weeks for delivery.

Prices subject to change without notice.